"[Kerri Pomarolli] is clean, bright, and funny. She's the girl you'd want for a daughter, the big sister you wish your teenager had to look up to. How does she thrive in the not-too-nice world of comedy professionals? Somebody up there likes her. So do we!"

Terry Meeuwsen and Louise DuArt
Hosts of *Living the Life Television*, CBN,
ABC Family

"Amazingly REAL! Kerri's hilarious approach to life teaches us all that there is incredible freedom when we take off our Christian masks and learn to laugh at ourselves! I LOVED this book!"

Erin Campbell
Host and Executive Producer of *Water through the Word* Radio for Women

"This book from page to page is classic. Kerri's natural wit, talent for self examination, and unparallel ability to laugh at herself makes this book a page-turner from beginning to end. Her heart to seek the best God has for her and point others in that same direction makes this a must-read for anyone who is struggling with their singlehood. You will laugh, you will cry, and most important, you will see the heart of God in Kerri's book."

Debbie Fuller
Christian Hollywood Magazine

"Kerri's use of real-time life experiences with her combination of honesty and humor were a relief to my heart. Uplifting and a breath of fresh air, Kerri's vulnerability and style calls it like it is and provides a lighthearted look at a true personal relationship with a real and ever-loving Father. It is a must-read."

Karyn A. Long
Cofounder of After Eve, A Young
Women's Conference

"[*Guys Like Girls Named Jennie* is] for anyone who avoids the how-to books (like me) and craves an honest, fresh, and funny perspective from the trenches. A page-turner for all women, this book is witty, engaging, and hopeful."

Monika Moreno
Director of the Angelus Awards
Student Film Festival

"I was so excited to finally read a Christian singles book that I could relate to. Kerri Pomarolli was open and honest about her struggles, and I really appreciate that. She showed both her challenges and her triumph. It made me feel like I was okay even though I face some of the same challenges. She is truly a joy and I'm so thankful that God brought this book in my path!"

Antique Book Reviews

guys like girls named
jennie

Formerly titled If I'm Waiting on God, Then What Am I Doing in a Christian Chatroom?

guys like girls named
jennie

kerri pomarolli

ZONDERVAN®

ZONDERVAN.com/
AUTHORTRACKER
follow your favorite authors

ZONDERVAN®

Guys Like Girls Named Jennie
Copyright © 2006 by Kerri Pomarolli

Originally published by Portley House Publishing 2004

Requests for information should be addressed to:
Zondervan, *Grand Rapids, Michigan* 49530

ISBN 978-0-310-28785-8

Interior design by Beth Shagene

Printed in the United States of America

08 09 10 11 12 13 14 • 23 22 21 20 19 18 17 16 15 14 13 12 11 10 9 8 7 6 5 4 3 2 1

To everyone who has ever failed the eHarmony® quiz

contents

with gratitude ...

There are so many people that deserve to be thanked. I can't even begin to mention you all by name, but please know I am so grateful for your encouragement and support.

First of all, to Rhonda Boudreaux, the best publicist/friend/ "mom" anyone could ask for! Thanks for fueling my email addiction and my career! Kathleen Boyle, my first editor, who gave so much to this project, and Doreen Hanna who gave us our connection. To Angela and the Zondervan team. Thank you for believing in my crazy message! To my other editors, Alexis, M. Wales, Chelsey Meek, Kristina Sword, and Kelsey Kirkandal. My "Mighty Women" who have prayed without ceasing and all my email prayer warriors. To my parents who said "Yes, you can!" and paid for all my lessons! To Mark, my brother, and my family for sitting through all my recitals! Thanks to my KHC family, the "woman Cathy," Maritza, Act in Faith, coach Kathleen, Kalina, Tiffini, and my CA family, the Cho's, who taught me how to use chopsticks, the Alpha Phi girls, "Gayle" in Grand Rapids, Jay Pesek, Ms. Shaw, Christia Mantzke, rock star sister, Brian Goff, Owen Song, the girlfriends who believed in me, laughed and cried with me along the way, and read all my emails. To the original Culver City Bible study girls who said "Write this stuff down!" And last, but certainly not least, to my very best friend, comedian Ron McGehee, who makes me tea and taught me that prayer works!

1

beginnings

While enjoying some cheese dip at a ladies' church function, I sat down near two twentysomething girls and noticed they were not wearing rings on their left ring fingers. *Great,* I thought to myself, *I'm not alone.* I was ready to meet some nice single girls and actually have a conversation that did not involve homeschooling or breast-feeding. I approached them and we introduced ourselves. My track record at church ladies' functions had involved a lot of craft circles and lectures on the benefits of making the perfect Christmas tree ornament out of old dried flowers. I was basically just there for the free food.

Jennifer told me she had just moved from Wisconsin to California and was staying with her boyfriend's parents until she found a place of her own. She briefly described her relationship: "It has been five months, and he is just the greatest," she said in that totally-in-love, high-pitched, sickeningly happy girlie voice.

I asked where she met him, and she smiled and shot her friend a knowing look. They both giggled and I immediately jumped in with, "The internet?"

"Why yes!" they laughed. "How did you know?" She went on to

tell me how she logged on to a Christian dating site where she met "Mr. Right." And just like that, she's in California!

"Well, that's great. I tried the online thing and ended up with a stalker. The police were involved and everything—it was so amazing!" I said with a huge smile and more than a hint of sarcasm. I then told them I was writing a book about my experience. After hearing the title, they were not too impressed. Were there any single women left on the planet who hadn't fallen prey to the world of internet dating? Had everyone sold out like me?

I went home and dove into a bag of potato chips and some chocolate chip cookies for comfort. That was supposed to be me, not Jennifer! With the click of my mouse I was going to design my husband. Kind of like that 80s movie *Weird Science* where two guys had the bright idea to design the perfect woman on their computer and then watch her magically appear before their eyes. They ended up with Kelly LeBrock and that ain't bad. What a great concept! I mean, I had tried everything else—well, almost everything. Why not embrace our world of technology?

Let's talk about dating. Oooohhhh, did I say a bad word? Do I believe in the pagan ritual of ... dare I say it again ... *dating*? Well, do I? Do you? I mean, did the powers-that-be leave out of the Bible the apostle Paul's letters to the Americans? I'll listen to them. But seriously, the world has all these rules about dating—what to do ... what to wear ... what not to wear—and I'm confused! I know dating is a very vital part of our culture today, and I know God has an opinion. He wants my heart to be pure, among other things. Yeah, well I do too! Where's the discrepancy? Oh yeah, it's when I watch too many romance movies and start to take dating tips from Meg Ryan that all chaos breaks loose.

You know, I've actually looked up "courtship" and "dating" in a Bible concordance and they were not there. There are no little notes in red on the side of my Bible that tell me anything about this concept at all. I think people in the Bible turned twelve and were magically married by God or by their parents—case closed. Of course, I can't let it go, so I read the next best thing ... every self-help book available to today's woman: *I Kissed Dating Goodbye, I Gave Dating a Chance, Boundaries in Dating, Loving Your Husband* (if I ever get one) Bible study, *The Power of a Praying Wife, Saving Your Marriage Before It Starts* ... Ha! Obviously *way* before it starts! Yes, I became a self-help junkie.

So I read all these self-help books because I'm a planner and because I figured there was a blueprint in them somewhere for the perfect relationship. If Oprah wasn't advertising any Christian dating books, I'd have to find the best ones myself. I know you laugh, but these books are addictive—and all along the Bible was sitting right there in front of me, patiently waiting to be opened. And don't you think my Father God was, and still is, patiently waiting for me to talk to him about it? I have asked the opinions of 175 strangers, acquaintances, pastors, mentors, and friends ... but not of God. That would be too easy! He is just sitting up there in heaven saying, "Would you please let me handle this?" He then waits for my response. And then he waits some more—years, in some cases. He is such a gentleman and will not intrude unless asked, and then ... look out! God takes over and life is never the same. I've learned that it is a powerful prayer when we actually ask God to get involved in our lives. I did just that and this is my story—before and after.

I'm not a teacher or a preacher, and I don't believe this book has the answers to life's great spiritual truths. This is not a "how-to anything" book. Maybe it's more along the lines of "how-not-to." This book was written in the moment, as much as possible, so I could portray the emotions going on in my crazy little head as they happened. No matter what your spiritual beliefs or background, I hope my story can speak to you, and when you take my journey with me, we can laugh along the way. Remember, if you doubt that God has a sense of humor, you haven't read about my love life yet!

As I reveal the blunders in all areas of my life, my hope is that you will be able to grasp how loving, patient, and gracious our God really is. In my life it is God who has been doing the waiting. He's been waiting for me to screw up enough times in order for me to realize I can't do this alone. I can't be a "do-it-yourself Christian." It doesn't work. It's hard and God doesn't want my life to be a series of mishaps. So he just loves me, gently prods me, and waits.

2

cleaning therapy

We all have different ways of coping with being alone—none is better or worse than the other. While I tend to call everyone in my phone directory, my friend isolates herself and turns to compulsive cleaning. Alas, why can't she come have a breakdown at my place?

It's not like there aren't biblical coping mechanisms right there at our fingertips. But nooo, we'd rather use our fingertips to dial the phone and call thirteen of our closest friends to ask for advice, or we dive into compulsive behaviors. My friend once said, "Once you finish compulsively cleaning your apartment and making it perfect, all your issues will still be there." Yeah, I've never struggled with that.

I'm an advice addict. I love to seek counsel—some wise, some not-so-wise, and some totally out of the ballpark, just for drama. My conversations usually go something like this: "Hey, it's Kerri! How are you? Good? Good. Um, me? Oh, I'm great. Just busy runnin' around like crazy. Why? Oh, there's just a lot going on in my life. Like what? Well … it all started last week …" And then I proceed to tell my latest sob story with no detail left untold. I want my friend to get the *whole* picture.

I have the ability to re-create entire conversations—voices and all—just to get the full effect. I also have the ability to make my counselor-of-the-minute feel like my supreme mentor. I'd say, "So what do you think? Wow! You're amazing. I knew I couldn't go to anyone but you. You have really helped me get some clarity. Thanks." Click ... dial another number.

Little did they know I was taking the thirty-one-flavors approach to counseling. Variety is the spice of life, right? I'm unable to decide if what I craved more was the attention or the validation. This dependency on over-the-phone counseling became so debilitating; I was unable to make a decision on anything of importance without the consultation of my tribal council. This group consisted of my parents, two guys I dated in college, two guys I was close pals with at the time, my roommate, faraway school pals, old friends from near and far, women I know and respect in my church, women I don't know that well but respect in my church, my mentor Maritza, and last but not least, Harold, my building manager and second dad. When he stopped by to change a lightbulb, he was forced into therapy. I actually think he somewhat enjoyed it. Harold would shake his head and laugh at me — pretty much in the same manner Ricky Ricardo reacted when Lucy got herself into another mess.

I know there has got to be a better way, but I haven't found it yet. My Bible doesn't talk back when I read it ... but Harold does and my mother and friends do, so I'm forced to listen to their opinions. If there was a talking Bible that gave advice ... now that would be really cool!

3

boys like girls
named jennie

I'm at a weird place right now. I'm not dating or even interested in anyone. It's the first time in twenty years; I even had a boyfriend in kindergarten — Brandon Duck. During recess we would say "I love you" with our hands crossed over our hearts. We even got in trouble for holding hands on the Amtrak train field trip to Canada. I wish my mom hadn't been chaperoning *that* one! Of course he moved on to Jennie Grabda in second grade, and I was left out in the cold. All the boys liked Jennie; she was cute and tan and brunette, and I … well, I talked too much.

I used to pray every night, "Dear God, let me kiss a boy. Please, God, please." That kiss didn't happen until I went through a million grade school love affairs and was 14 ½ years old. It was in Boston at the Ford Auto Show my parents had brought me to. His name was Todd Kramer and that first kiss took place while we were sitting and playing the Pole Position game. (I know there are those of you reading this who are old enough to remember Pole Position and Atari. And if you're not, I don't want to hear it!) The kiss was wet and sloppy and not at all what I expected, but I did it anyway. My emotions just took off.

That night Todd and I decided we were soul mates and destined to be married. He told me I was the prettiest girl in the world and promised to buy me an island in Jamaica where we could live and we'd fly there on his plane. The thing is, he came from the kind of family that owned planes and boats, so that sort of promise didn't seem too far-fetched.

I remember writing in my diary, "I love Todd. He's 5' 6 ½" and strong." He promised we would stay together forever! When I think about it, this was one of my very first do-it-yourself moments. I'd been praying and waiting for this moment, and when it came I just took the bull by the horns and went for it. Though I didn't initiate it, to this kiss is what I compared all the others. Todd set the stan-dard—if you're going to do something intimate like kiss someone, there better be intentions behind it, like an "I love you" or a marriage proposal. Which is probably why I'm still single.

That week we proceeded to be joined at the hip, not to mention lips, and professed our love for each other hourly. This affair con-sisted of sharing cotton candy and kielbasa sausages, holding hands, and most important, finding hiding spots to perfect our lip-locking. This time was so exhilarating I could barely sleep, much less notice our parents' utter dismay at our behavior. I think they were stunned and hoped it would pass.

After the exchange of such personal items as my sunglasses and his Ford pin, we departed with a tearful, dramatic goodbye and set out to return to our respective lives in Michigan and Missouri. I thanked God for bringing me my husband and then proceeded to write Todd an eight-page letter expressing my complete despair at being apart from him.

We wrote, we made audiotapes, and we called and called. I think one of my phone bills was over four hundred dollars. (This was be-fore the days of ten cents a minute and free nights and weekends.) I don't even remember what we talked about, but we probably were reliving our glorious week together, telling each other how miser-able we were to be apart. And of course, we each said we were being "faithful" … which I was *not*. I mean, really! It was ninth grade and I needed a date for homecoming. What, are you crazy? You think I'd stay home and miss the chance to wear all that taffeta? No way! Yet I practiced writing "Kerri Kramer" and "Mrs. Kramer" in English class every chance I got. The teacher even kicked me out of class for daydreaming. That's okay though, because I got out of trouble by making up some sob story about problems at home and my teacher bought it; I was good at that.

I know I prayed to God about my life, but it was more like: "Dear God, thank you for this day. Thank you for Todd. Please let him come to visit. And please let me make the cheerleading squad. Amen." By the way, he did let me make the cheerleading squad, but it wasn't junior varsity so I quit. Details, Kerri, details! I forgot to say JV in my prayers!

Now I had officially entered the world of romance. Of course, I had been there all my life but now there were actually boys involved. I was so boy crazy growing up. Even my friends' parents noticed it and thought I was a little cuckoo. No matter, I persevered in search of my prince.

I went to a small, and I mean *small*, Christian school (Dutch Reformed). Dad was Catholic and made sure I faithfully attended catechism and Mass each Sunday. During those years I didn't learn much about boys in school *or* in church. However, I did learn about sex: Don't do it before you're married or you'll go to hell. Plain and simple. That was the rule in my house. It worked too! No need for discussion. *And* I knew I wasn't allowed to date until I was sixteen.

But that rule didn't stop me. My best friend Jennie Sollars and I cruised the neighborhood on our ten-speed bicycles looking for guys. All the boys liked Jennie; I was just the tagalong friend hoping to get some guy's attention. We'd rendezvous with them at the ice cream store. Well, at least it was a planned meeting on our part; most of the time the boys weren't aware of much.

Occasionally, several boys would ride by Jennie's house where we had planted ourselves on the porch, waiting for them for hours. When they rode by it was usually our cue to run home and pick up the phone and call them. And say what? Nothing really. It was more about the calling process and then giggling afterward. We'd pick two friends and try to get them to ask us to "go out." We didn't actually *go* anywhere. That was not required to hold the title of "going out." Mainly, the idea behind the concept was to have a name to fill in the blank of "I love _____." Even still, my southern mother's only advice was "Don't call boys" or "Don't chase boys." Wow! How crazy was she? I was a new woman of the 1980s! What did she know? Life was like an episode of *The Wonder Years.* I miss those days when a boy riding a bike by my house was my idea of exciting. Who am I kidding? A boy riding by my house now would still be exciting! My, how some things never change.

4

i love corey feldman

As I evaluate the behavior of my adolescent years, I realize I was just waiting for "Mr. Right Now" in a proactive way … just as we women do now. I'd make it particularly easy for a boy to grab my attention. In fact, the boys didn't have to do much at all, other than acknowledge my existence as a woman—I'd do the rest by creating the fantasy romance in my pretty little head and then share all the exaggerated details with my friends.

Sound familiar? How many mediocre-to-bad relationships have you sugarcoated to your friends just to make yourself look good and feel better? Okay, some of us take the "drama queen" option, relaying every sordid, miserable detail of our relationships to our friends in a cry for advice, when really we just want to be validated and told we're right and that we're better than him.

These behavior patterns develop early on in life. Think back to junior high or high school. Were you the girl who had it all together and was always "fine"? Were you the one everyone leaned on for support, comfort, and advice? Little did they know you were just as insecure and clueless about the opposite sex as they were. But maybe you grew up watching a lot of TV and learned valuable dating tips from *Ricki Lake* or *Beverly Hills 90210*. Let's not underestimate the power and effect TV has on us and our views regarding dating and men. How many young girls across America thought sex before marriage was not okay unless it was (a) prom night or (b) your date got a hotel room like Dylan and Brenda on *90210*? Then it was more than okay! Admit it—you know who you are.

Once in seventh grade (when I was way too old to be lying), I told my friends that my dad fixed me up with Corey Feldman (the actor in *Goonies*) and that he was my boyfriend. Those Dutch Reformed kids would believe anything! I had to do it—it was too easy. The stories I made up weren't always about my love life. I was telling stories even as far back as kindergarten. When my aunt would sometimes drop me off for school in her Cadillac, I told everyone she was our chauffeur. That didn't go over well at parent's night. Creating these stories became so easy I almost started believing them myself. Anything for attention, I guess. I know God was up there laughing his head off thinking, *My little storyteller. Keep on spinning those tales, honey, because you're in for a long ride.*

If only I had known! Even back then I didn't have faith that God was concerned with my love life. He was just some omnipotent being up there making me feel guilty for things I would get caught doing. I was in charge of my life and my actions, and when I got scared a few times, I would turn to him in prayer. After all, I studied the Bible six days a week—you would think some of it might have sunk in! It did eventually, but not until fifteen years later.

5

daddy's girl

Today I was going through my "dad cards" that hang on the wall. I have the greatest dad in the world. No one can touch him. I get homemade greeting cards every day. Yes, you read that right. Every day. Don't ask—I've never figured it out either. I've been getting them since college. When I'm lucky, there will also be a five-dollar bill in the envelope. That's one of his ways of showing me he loves me and cares about me. When I was in college I didn't have my own car, so Dad would send me five-dollar bills for cab fare because it was too cold for his "baby" to walk to class in the snow in Michigan. I think I'll even start a scholarship someday for a lucky sorority girl at my college and provide her with cab fare every day for four years in honor of my dad.

I put the special cards up on my wall. Some have been there for years. Sometimes he watches too many *Godfather* movies and signs them "Mafia Dad" or "Italian Wisdom Dad." He's so creative, and these cards have become a blessing and a staple in my daily life. In times of darkest trouble I could always count on going to the mailbox and seeing a homemade card from my dad, with the perfect saying to cheer me up or some funny cartoon he cut out for me. Mostly his messages were telling me to never give up on my dreams and that he supported me and loved me. Sometimes those were the only things that kept me from packing it up out here in Hollywood where I now live and moving home to get a "real job"!

I was looking through them today, and a couple of the cards had faded so badly I couldn't read the messages he had written. I took them down and decided to trace over the words. As I was doing this, God was showing me that his unending love for me as my heavenly Father will never fade. He loves me and cares for me eternally. He may not tell me through cards, but he finds ways to tell me every single day. For starters, he speaks to me through my earthly dad. If I take the time to look around, God is telling me things every single day through people in my life, his Word, the beauty he has created on this earth for me to enjoy, and a million little things like "free manicure" coupons in the mail. God so wants to give me what my heart desires — if I would quit stepping in and trying to fulfill those desires myself, which we know is an unending quest!

band-aids and shortcuts

I heard a story from my friend Linda tonight as we got together at her house to pray. She had a girlfriend who was in a terrible accident as a teenager. Her face was smashed into the gravel pavement and a lot of gravel was imbedded in her cheek. Her doctor said there were two routes. The first route was to put a bandage on it and let it heal with the gravel still there. It wouldn't hurt, but she would be scarred for life. The second route was to do a deep peeling of the layers of her skin. It would be long and painful, but in the end she would have new, baby soft skin and no scars. She chose route two.

How many of us will let God peel away the gravel in our lives? Or do we want the painless way that seems easier at the time but leaves scars forever? Sometimes we let God start to remove a layer of skin in order to release the gravel, but it hurts too much, so we just slap a Band-Aid on our cheek and walk away. God never said trusting and surrendering everything would be easy. It wasn't easy for Abraham when God told him to leave his family and go out alone. God didn't even tell him where to go! Are we so different? Why are we so much more special? God knows what his desires are for our lives, but will we ever find out? Not unless we trust him implicitly.

Like the time I was on vacation with my friends in St. Thomas, and we were staying in a condo. I immediately found out where the Ritz Carlton was, and when my girlfriends were out hiking or biking, I would sneak into their pool and beach club like I was a guest and enjoy the fancy chairs and cabana boys without paying the hefty price tag. It was both luxurious and free! It was where I felt most comfortable. My bank account has not caught up with my lifestyle choices yet, so I had to find the shortcut.

My mom and I even snuck into a fancy pool when we were in Hawaii and got caught. The pool attendant asked my name, and I panicked and looked at him in my most serious James Bond way and said, "Smith ... Jaclyn Smith." Well, I didn't look like a Charlie's Angel, so we were busted. I've had a lifetime of experiences trying to take the shortcut and some are harmless. But when it comes to what kind of relationships we're going to have, are we going to take the road less traveled and "wait on God" or are we going to date anyone who comes our way just because we want the "free dinner" and some company on a Friday night? Remember, nothing is ever really free! Trust me — I've been kicked out of some of the finest hotels in the world.

7

working out and
other miseries

I just came back from beach boot camp and found myself racing around all morning. I didn't make it through the beach workout because I was hot. I hate sweating!

Kind of like my life. I've always felt like I was in some race: a race to get married, the Hollywood rat race, and now the race to spiritual enlightenment. Well, God wants us to run the race, but it's not the kind we think it is. It's running the race with God to do his powerful work on this earth. And when I want to turn back, relax, and get my nails done, he gently says, "Come on, Kerri! Don't turn back now. It's just a few more steps. You can do it." He's right! I can, and I'm learning that everything is possible through Christ who strengthens me … whether it is on a physical, emotional, or spiritual level. He gives us the perseverance to draw nearer to him and to become stronger in the process.

I hate working out. I mean, I live in LA. We drive to get the mail! I've tried every kind of workout: the gym—a two-year membership and I think I went twice; the personal trainer—expensive and I chatted my way out of working out; Tae-Bo videos; Richard Simmons' *Sweatin' to the Oldies*—even the fifty-year-olds were killing me; *Buns of Steel*; Pilates; and yoga with the senior citizens. Some of those eighty-year-olds were in much better shape than me, but we all enjoyed the buffet after class. You get my drift. I could never commit, and Pizza Hut on my couch won every time.

Having that personal relationship with God reminds me of working out. It's something so good for me and so simple, but I've made it so hard and complicated. Like I said before, I've read every Christian book about "knowing God," and every Christian bestseller, when what God really wants from me is some of my time—consistent time—every day. And what do I get in return? The reward is my spirit getting stronger and being more able to resist temptations, like having more patience with my mother when she calls me and her first question is always "Did you meet anyone?" She calls me every day, every hour on the hour with the same question!

On the few occasions where I've put this into practice and actually taken the time to read the Bible and pray, I have a sense of well-being throughout my day. One time I even wrote down my "To Do" list and prayed about each silly little thing. It may seem like small stuff, but God does sweat the small stuff and he wants to help me all day long. The thing is that those days are so great that I think I don't need to pray again for help the next morning, and it turns into a vicious cycle. I'm learning though—I really am!

8

diva on a mission

I believe everything in life can be a learning experience. Right now I'm on an official church-sponsored mission trip to Mississippi.

I tried this mission thing two years ago when I went to be a counselor at a summer camp for Los Angeles foster kids. Let's just say I'm not exactly the camper or kid-friendly type. I love kids, but I've never really been around them, so I couldn't understand why a five-year-old couldn't put on her own shoes. Or why I had to tie them. Also, the whole "getting in the pool thing" didn't work for me. I didn't want to get my hair wet, but I had to convince the other counselors that I was participating. I'd sit on the edge of the pool, pretending to get in every few minutes, and also convincing my campers it was for their protection; I stayed by the side so I could watch them better. I told them, "Kids, it's like the *Wizard of Oz*. Counselor Kerri will melt if she gets her hair wet!" That week was a challenge and every day I thought I might not make it to the next. It was hot and muggy and our cabins had bugs in them and my campers weren't as into "nap time" as I was. Actually, there was no nap time—I just made it up, but they weren't buying it!

Anyway, I survived camp and it truly was an amazing experience emotionally. God knew my laziness so well that one of my campers cancelled at the last minute, so instead of two campers I only had one sweet little girl to look after. We got along great and shared a cabin with five other campers and two other counselors.

Okay, so I decided to try a different kind of mission trip this time. I convinced the team leader from my church that I could cook, so I was assigned to the kitchen crew for a work trip in Jackson, Mississippi. Twenty or so of us went down to rebuild houses for people in need. I also figured this would be a good way to actually learn to cook because the other ladies would know what they were doing. And that part had been great. I didn't mind being up at 5:30 a.m. and scrambling eggs. It's just that everyone here works so hard doing all the physical labor that I don't find appealing in the least. So I avoid doing any physical work by volunteering to run to the store all the time.

I suppose I'd consider myself somewhere between totally self-serving and lazy—or maybe I'm just environmentally challenged. I really hate physical labor—anything that makes me sweat, actually. Am I spoiled and lazy? Even Betty, an eighty-seven-year-old woman here with us, takes fewer naps than I do. It's terrible.

Yesterday we were reading 2 Timothy 3, about the last days on earth before Christ returns, in which it talks about people being pleasure seekers and lovers of money. That really hit home. All I could think about were the sweet people here in Mississippi who barely had enough money for food and shelter, and then there's little ol' me obsessing over which colors to paint my wicker chairs in my new beach house that I know God is going to give me soon. I'm serious and I don't know how to stop. I kept getting enticed by magazines at the checkout counter called *Country Cottage*, with articles like "101 Ways to Paint a Porch Floor" or "How to Stretch Your Decorating Dollars." It's pathetic.

I returned to my room and cried out to God to give me a servant's heart. Sometimes it's so hard to do things that are laborious, but I'm sure there's some satisfaction to it. I did glue some shells on a mirror today. Does that count? I just get so down on myself because I try to play it off like I'm this midwestern girl who's so down to earth, but really I'm not too far down there—not far enough to get my hands in the dirt. It's not that I'm high maintenance either. I just keep praying God will give me more energy and a better attitude. I hope he does before I become a mom someday, because somebody is going to have to chase after those kids and tie their shoes and stuff!

9

ya gotta have a gimmick

You have to love my dad. He loves to buy presents. Last Christmas he gave me a beautiful necklace with a silver *M* on it and my full name is Kerri Lynn Pomarolli. Yep, I was confused. I asked him what the *M* was for and he said, "Michigan!"

I grew up in Michigan and also went to college there. My dad is too cute. So of course I wear it and sure enough friends will always ask, "Um, Kerri, why are you wearing an *M*?" I usually tell the story about my dad, or if it's a stranger I'll act like a dumb blonde, smile, and say, "*M* is for me." If a single guy asks about the *M*, I say, "*M* is for marriage." I love to see the look on their faces. It truly gives me joy to see them squirm.

The necklace is always a good conversation starter—which reminds me of my days back in college going to frat parties. I had this huge silver bear I would wear around my neck. And no, it wasn't sexy. My girlfriends would make fun of me. But guess what happened as soon as we arrived at these so-called mixers? None of the guys would approach the girls until one guy would stumble over and say, "Uh ... nice bear!"

Well, the line may not be Shakespeare, but that was when I figured out that I needed to have a gimmick to get a guy's attention.

It was back when women's ties were in style. And sure enough, if I wore a tie, one of these same guys would come over and make some brilliant comment like, "Hey, I like your tie," which would launch one of those deeply intellectual conversations that were commonly held at these parties over the keg as the Prince music set the tone in the background. Ah ... the best of times!

Eventually, we'd be on the dance floor strutting our awesome moves to "Let's Go Crazy." Wow! I was a hit ... and all because of accessories. Wasn't God proud? I had it all figured out at the ripe old age of nineteen! Plaid pants, ties, bear necklaces ... I was famous for my conversation starters. One fraternity actually referred to me as the "girl in the red plaid pants." Years later I was told they were quite flattering in that tight "I need attention" kind of way. Like my mom always said when it comes to fashion, "More is more!" My friends laugh about it to this day.

Now when I go to a new place or meeting, I like to wear one of my beautiful crosses. Sometimes they start some good conversations, but I don't wear a cross as a gimmick; it's a symbol of what I believe in and a part of who I am. And I'm more than happy to share that with anyone who asks me about it. Another thing I know is that when I meet the man God has for me, it won't be because of a necklace. (It'll probably be because of my hair.)

As I look back on all my adventures in Dating Land and what I did to get the attention of the opposite sex — big hair, small pants, etc. — I know I would do things differently, but I wouldn't want to skip the process entirely. We learn from our mistakes and find out more about who we are, right? If someone had told me when I was fifteen that dating wasn't important, I would have laughed. Boys = life! We live in an obsessed world where princes marry young maidens, solve all their problems, and buy them a castle in which they never do housework, and all the men are polite, handsome, and good dancers. Who wouldn't want that? You can try to hide TV, movies, and fairy tales from your kids, take them out of public school, and not let them look at beauty magazines and billboards, but let's get real. We can't shelter our little girls forever. I'm not sure what the answer is.

I think I did all those crazy things because I didn't know much about my Father God and the real gifts he had for me. I wish someone had sat me down and really talked to me about purity and true love, and why waiting to give my heart away to one special man was the greatest gift I could offer. Waiting, to me, was a decision based on fear, not a choice made out of obedience to God, knowing the abundant blessings I would receive in the end. Yes, I'm still waiting on all of them.

I hate reading Christian books that are all about waiting on God and how hard it is, and then I come to find out the author has been happily married since she (or he) was nineteen! Doesn't it seem like all Christians get married right after puberty? I mean, if you're twenty-five, a Christian, and single, people need to be lifting you up in prayer — as my mother and her friends have been doing for years. "Oh Lord, please find a husband for Kerri and please let him have a job with health insurance." (Yeah, we set the standard really high in my family.) I just want other women to believe in God's perfect timing. No matter where you are or where you've been, it's never too late to commit yourself to the Lord and let him handle everything in your life.

10

you would be so nice to come home to

As I came in late last Saturday night—since God has not given me an adoring husband to greet me—I found myself seeking the comfort that my refrigerator has to offer. I don't even think I was hungry, but it's a habit I've developed. I scanned the shelves and went directly to the freezer and pulled out a pint of mint chocolate chip. I put it next to the chocolate syrup that was still sitting out from the binge I had earlier.

It occurred to me that I buy "make-me-happy" foods like ice cream (the real stuff: Ben and Jerry's Chocolate Mint Chunk, 48 grams of fat, 1,888 carbs) and potato chips—anything with lots of sugar or salt. I try to trick myself and buy sugar-free ice cream and nonfat tofu ice cream sandwiches. It works for about a minute, but then my brain realizes what I'm trying to do and it revolts. I go back to the fridge searching for something to really fill my hunger. I've trained my body to accept nothing less than the things I deem acceptable. I try to eat the edamame—and in theory it does taste okay by itself—but I find it goes really well with Doritos and Hostess cupcakes. Those Hostess cupcakes aren't just for kids, I tell ya. I can go back to blaming my sugar addiction on my childhood that was filled with every delicious, artificially flavored treat imaginable.

My mother thought Froot Loops was a healthy breakfast, God bless her! This is also the woman who weighs a whopping 105 pounds and complains that she can't gain weight no matter what she eats. Why didn't I inherit that gene?

The bottom line is that I'm trying to re-train my brain and tell it that sugar-free pudding is yummy and so is diet soda. I mean, swimsuit season is coming and unfortunately I ain't sixteen anymore. I can't buy the "good" stuff or have it in sight; otherwise, I'll eat it … and fast. This comes from a long family tradition of ice cream sundaes every night before bed. That is one of the ways my family bonds: We eat and we shop and then we eat some more! Hey … we're Italian!

Oreos last about twenty-four hours in my apartment. I'll even get up at three in the morning and stumble into the kitchen in my daze and polish off a few, sending the message to my system, "It's okay, Kerri, we have Oreos; you can go back to sleep." That only triggers me to go for the ice cream right out of the carton for breakfast at 8:30 a.m. And since I don't live with my parents anymore, I can do that with little guilt.

So why does food make us feel better? What makes me go directly for the cabinets of cookies and chips when I walk in my door? It's learned behavior and I have to stop saying, "Chocolate makes me happy" and instead say, "Thin thighs make me happy." I haven't come close to mastering it yet. I've tried all sorts of methods. Like the time I saw the no carb, no calorie, no fat gummi bears and bought a bag. I started munching on them in my car, and they weren't half bad. In half an hour they were gone, but I had no guilt. I just should have read the fine print on the package: "Excessive consumption may cause a laxative effect." May cause? MAY CAUSE? How about, "Watch out kiddies, you're in for a bumpy ride!" I thought I was going to die. I was sure it was food poisoning. I prayed a lot that day. Once again, I learned if it looks too good to be true—for the last time—it probably is! There are no calorie-free lunches.

So it is in my walk with Christ. I can't do my one-minute devotionals and expect to be spiritually fed and grounded for the day. As a Catholic, I thought I had it down — forty-five minutes a week, a few songs, an "Our Father," a fifteen-minute sermon, and I'm outta there. When I was a kid, I used to brag about the priest at my church who gave ten-minute sermons and how he was great because he could get the job done quicker than anyone else.

Church for me was just showing up, checking in, and doing my time. God doesn't want that from me. He wants a relationship. He wants me to enjoy reading his Word. He wants to take the place of worldly comforts. That's a hard lesson to learn. How could God comfort my hunger? But didn't Jesus say in John 7:37–38, "If anyone is thirsty, let him come to me and drink. Whoever believes in me, as the Scripture has said, streams of living water will flow from within him"? He was always caring for people, turning water into wine, feeding the crowd with loaves and fishes. But he also fills that hunger inside of us that no chocolate sundae can satisfy. Trust me. He knows our needs — he invented chocolate sundaes and it's all good. But the Lord wants to give us the sustenance we are lacking deep down inside our souls. He'll do it too, but we have to ask and seek and know him.

He's waiting for us every morning and he's still there as we drift off to sleep. I can see him up there, longing to help me carry all the burdens of my busy day, but I'm too busy being busy to ask to be fed and helped. So now I'm trying to read the Bible; it's becoming a "make-me-happy" food for my soul. I'm working on it and I'll get there ... besides, it has no calories!

11

why can't i just ask
for directions?

Why is feeling God's presence in my life so hard? Am I missing the signs? I try so hard, even though I know that won't do it. How can someone like me learn to rest and actually feel God's arms wrapped around me? I'm so sick of hearing Christians telling me to "Rest in God! Rest in God!" when the world keeps telling me to "Go, go, go—do something—save the world—make a difference—save the whales—go to school—study hard—get a good job—stay busy—fill your time with activities and causes—and you'll be satisfied." I tried all of that, and I'm still yearning for more. I just can't read any more books on finding God's love.

So do I need a road map? Well yes, that would be nice. It could be a treasure hunt like in my favorite movie *The Goonies*, where they go underground in search of pirate treasure as they are chased by the mean Fratellis. (Note: If you haven't already, see that movie. My boyfriend from seventh grade, Corey Feldman, is in it.) In my treasure hunt, I find God's unconditional love, the feeling that I'm doing what he wants. If he were here he would say, "Well done, good and faithful servant."

I keep writing the word *feeling*, which leads me to believe I'm being led by my emotions on this topic. Alas, we women do that, don't we? We're such feeling-oriented creatures and God created us that way. I just don't want to get too caught up "feeling" everything rather than experiencing it fully with my heart and mind. I lay in my bed staring at the ceiling and trying to hear God's voice or feel his presence. It never works when I'm concentrating. I secretly pray, "Dear God, can I pllleeease hear your voice audibly just one time? Could I please have an angel come down next to my bed right now—just one time—I promise, God! That would be so cool!" God just doesn't work like that. I think if I spent more time reading his Word and meditating on it I would feel better. But I don't meditate. I'm like the scurried rabbit from *Alice in Wonderland.* "I'm late. I'm late for a very important date ... with my TV ... my computer ... some guy I just met." You know the drill. I thought about going to one of those silent retreats where you just pray, but I might literally drive myself mad, so for now I'm starting with as much quiet time as I can give every morning, and we'll see where we go from there.

12

mean reds

Do you ever get lonely inside for no reason? Life can be sailing along and sometimes I just wake up in a bad/sad mood that no amount of carbohydrates can cure. Audrey Hepburn in *Breakfast at Tiffany's* called it the "mean reds." I get the mean reds mixed with the green-with-envy blues. I see all my friends getting what they want, and it just seems easier for some people than others. I know I need to count my blessings and not feel sorry for myself, but there are days I just can't kick these feelings of self-pity—even sadness—because my life isn't moving along the way I planned it. I should have been married and on a sitcom by now. Life never does go like this, but I keep planning and plotting and scheming and dreaming. When will I learn that God has bigger and better plans for my life, so I can just relax and actually enjoy my days? I want to rest in God and trust him and walk in faith—seriously, I do. But I don't know how, or do I? Am I making it more complicated than God intended? Why does having faith seem so much easier for other people?

There's a fine line between walking in faith and being totally apathetic. I can relate to David when he cried out to God in the Psalms, as he saw his enemies prosper even though they were not God-fearing men. I keep thinking, *When will all my hard work pay off?* I mean, if we're all going to heaven, then do those who suffered for God get a better seat? Am I going to be right up there between the thief on the cross and Mother Teresa?

It's the Catholic in me—I want the point system so I can feel that my life and suffering, in the name of Jesus, is getting me something. This is sinful, I know, but I can't help thinking that way, and I just have to come to terms with the fact that there is no "point system" to serving God. We serve God because he died for us, gave us everlasting life, and because we love him. End of story.

I just have so many questions to ask when I meet him. Do you think there will be a Q & A in heaven where we all sit at God's feet and ask him everything we've ever wanted to know, or will that information be implanted in our brains upon arrival? Inquiring minds want to know! For instance … pantyhose. Were they really necessary?

13

why i don't watch chick flicks

You know, having God as my "boyfriend" has its perks—no one to fight with, he's always there listening to me, he's patient, kind, loving. You get the picture. Well, I was doing just fine with this concept and feeling good about life and myself, having that nice feeling that all is well. I wasn't looking for guys. I even went to a party on Saturday night not expecting to meet my future husband. Guess what? I didn't! I used to get ready to go out every weekend and just know that tonight was the night I was going to meet my Prince Charming. Why I thought we'd meet in some bar on the Hermosa Pier is beyond me. I did meet a lot of toads though. That's another book altogether. Okay, back to my point.

I came home tonight and made myself some dinner. Well, I did pour the chili out of the can and chop the onions, which was a big deal for me. I turned on the TV and began to watch *Bridget Jones' Diary.* I had seen it before and liked it. I guess I forgot that the last time I saw it I was a year younger *and* had a boyfriend! Anyway, it's about a thirty-two-year-old woman who calls herself a spinster and thinks she'll never get married. That doesn't keep her from trying though! She puts on the miniskirt and pursues an affair with the office scoundrel played by Hugh Grant. Let the sexual Olympics begin.

At this point in the movie I recognize this as wrong behavior (good job, Kerri) and know that this will only lead to heartbreak (which it does). What caught me by surprise is at the end of the movie, after all her bawdy behavior, Bridget ends up with a sweet, charming guy who adores her and is even better than the first one. And as they were passionately making out and the snow was falling, I got *so* depressed. I had forgotten what kissing looks like, and there it was staring me in the face, once again confirming that I am alone. It was too much to take.

I considered calling one of my "inner circle" for phone validation but resisted. Instead, I headed for the chocolate chip cookies that were hidden in my roommate's bedroom. She has them in her room because when she brought the first tub home I accidentally ate them all somewhere around 3:00 a.m. They sort of soothed my heart and stomach for a minute or two. But I just decided those chick flicks make me crazy. I mean the story usually goes like this: Girl meets boy, they laugh, they have an affair, he leaves, she cries and listens to bad love songs, either he comes back or she meets someone better, and all is well. Why can't life be like the movies? Not like *Casablanca* or anything that has a sad ending. But maybe just once, could John Cusack come over to my house and play Peter Gabriel on the radio below my window like in *Say Anything*.

I talk to God sometimes in my utter frustration and cry out to him, whining about my love life. He's the only one who really listens:

Dear God,

I know you know my heart and I'll admit it—I want the love story and I'm willing to wait on you and see who you have for me. But could you either hurry it up or really let me know he'll be worth the wait, because my poor mother Barbara is suffering from not

guys like girls named jennie

having any grandkids and she has no problem letting me know of her agony. You think it's easy listening to that? Every time I tell her I leave the house she asks, "Did you meet anyone?" I say, "Yeah mom! There was a doctor in my mailbox today when I went to get the mail and now I'm engaged!" She's shameless. Little miss "don't call boys" has certainly changed her tune. Well, kind of— she still holds true to that theory. She just assumes that some handsome man, a doctor preferably, will fall out of the sky as I'm getting my mail. Poor Barbara. See God, it's not just for me that I want to get married. I'm the only daughter, and I have a lot of people depending on me. I've gotten their hopes up sooo many times! And now I'm running around telling everyone I'm waiting on you to send me someone. I know you won't let me down. This time I might actually do the waiting part!

14

childhood memories

Today I came across some old diaries and books. I always loved to write. I even had my very own autograph book. I didn't know many famous people so I made up entries myself. One said, "To Kerri. You are my fav fan! Love, Mic Zany." I don't know where I came up with that name, but it sounded like someone famous. I also saw one saying, "To Kerri, my lovely sister. I love you. Love, Mark" in scribbled handwriting. My brother refused to sign it so I took the liberty of signing for him. I had my pretend boyfriends sign it too, so I could show it off to my friends in second grade. But I kept that book later on and had my castmates sign it when we did plays. I'd always have some backstage crush and getting him to sign my book was very dramatic. Jesse Rafferty was this cute and charming blue-eyed kid who could sing like an old-time movie star. One year we did a show together called *The Boyfriend* and he wrote in my book, "Kerri, great job. You're very talented and I loved working with you. You were the perfect Polly (my character) sweet, beautiful, and fun to be with. Love, Jesse." He was so sweet for a ninth grader, and I took that book home and read it over and over to myself planning our love affair that never materialized. I still cherish that book and those autographs.

I'm glad I wrote things as a kid. It's wonderful to look back on the fact that I was a total drama queen when I was eight and haven't changed much since then.

I found one of my first diary entries from third grade. It read: "Today Adam sat by me in reading lab. Keri Finlay likes Adam too. I wish she'd keep her claws off him. I have to wear these rollers in my hair to look good tomorrow." Remember the pink foam sponge rollers girls would wear overnight—no matter what amount of pain we'd experience—just to get that perfect head of bouncy curls? I didn't realize that getting a boy's attention motivated even that behavior.

Adam was in my class and, honestly, I don't even think he was ever nice to me. I remember I was enamored by him during kickball and soccer at recess. He would be downright mean, just like the other boys. They teased me mercilessly. I now know why. Most of the other girls would cry and then wouldn't get picked on. But I wasn't like the other girls. I was 4' 6" with a mouth the size of Manhattan and would fight back to the death. We went head-to-head with comments about each other's mothers and anything else you could imagine. If I had shut up, I'm sure it would have been much less brutal. But I guess I thought this kind of attention was better than no attention at all. How terrible is that?

Why couldn't the boys like me the way they liked Keri Finlay who was tall, tan, and had a bigger chest than all the other girls combined? No, I was a tomboy and pretty much treated as one of the boys. It did improve my dodgeball and verbal skills though.

They say all comedians or performers have troubled childhoods. I wonder how much trouble we brought on ourselves with our need for attention and our big mouths? God had to be having a ball watching me! I wonder if the angels in heaven would gather around to watch what kind of trouble my mouth would get me in today. Was it getting caught in one of my tall tales I told on the school yard, like the fact that my dad set me up with Corey Feldman? Or breaking my arm on a double-dog dare on the monkey bars? Writing a love note to Anthony Policello only to get it intercepted and read to the whole class by Mrs. Veenstra, my third grade teacher? Are they still entertained today? I'm sure it only gets better!

15

hold on to the nights

I said before that one of the best things about being single is the fact that you have as much free time as you want to do exactly what you want. I'm all for it except on Sundays. Those are the toughest days to be alone. As I watch all the families and couples go off after church to their activities, I remember having a boyfriend who would take me on long drives in his BMW on Sundays. We'd go look at fancy houses and pretend we had the money to afford them. It was fun and I liked playing the role of the trendy LA wife.

It's a quiet Sunday afternoon and I'm enjoying my singleness by cleaning my bathroom. Oh, the joys of being alone. Who said it couldn't be glamorous? I now have more time for laundry and movies on the Oxygen network. It's a mystery to me why the male gender can't appreciate a cinematic classic like *Dirty Dancing* the way we girls do. I mean, come on! "Dance with me ... here ... now!" Does it get any cooler than Patrick Swayze swaying shirtless in the hot summer heat with Otis Redding playing in the background?

Anyway, all of a sudden, in the middle of scrubbing my sink, I heard Richard Marx's timeless ballad, "Hold On to the Nights," and I was transported back to Boston where I first met Todd Kramer (my first love) and all the emotions that "our song" brought back.

It was instantaneous; I even got goose bumps. I was remembering those feelings of what I thought was love, passion, and longing; how I listened to love songs and could relate to every single, sappy word. I felt the artist's pain and sorrow at being separated from her true love. Remember, Todd lived in Missouri and I was living in Michigan when we met. We were every bit as tragic as Romeo and Juliet, except we had letters and four-hundred-dollar phone bills to get us through until we could plan our next meeting.

Throughout the years, even though we lived thousands of miles apart, we'd call each other on a whim when "Hold On to the Nights" would come on the radio. I think he said he was on a date once and heard it and got all nostalgic and sad. He told me it kinda ruined the mood. I just laughed, because I'm sure that had happened to me too. I still feel close to him even though it's been years since we last saw each other, and he's now married and I'm sure living his happy life in Missouri. He went to work for his father just like I knew he would. And I came to California just as planned. But we'll always have our memories.

God created us with these amazing senses that are just dying to be awakened. I find that those special moments are few and far between, only arising when something or someone stirs me up inside. God definitely stirs me, but then I let those feelings fade; I forget my First Love. I forget the passion I've felt for him when I would be excited about church and let his Spirit move me through music or his Word. When I first fell in love with God, I cried during worship at church almost every Sunday for a year. They actually had Kleenex in the aisles of the little church I was attending, and I assumed they were there just for me. I wasn't looking around to see who was there or wondering how I looked or planning my week. I was *right* there in his presence, allowing his Holy Spirit to overcome me and woo my heart, as only he can.

There were times when I really felt convicted about the pattern of sin in my life, and I'd get down on my knees and repent. I would feel as though a huge weight was lifted off my shoulders. I felt peace; I felt free. I was letting God be my First Love—the greatest romance my heart could ever desire. For a long time I'd go back to my old habits as soon as Sunday was over, but I'd be right back there again a week later on my knees; God was always happy to see me. I miss those times. They seem so far away.

Lately, when I am in church, I have found myself distracted and wondering if people are watching me. If I were to kneel, would they think I'm trying to show off? If I don't stand, do they think I'm apathetic? If I sing too loudly, am I trying to show off that musical theater degree? Don't think I'm not looking for guys in the pews who could potentially be "the one" either! I'm so overly conscious of *me* and what I'm doing that it totally takes the focus off why I'm even there in the first place ... to connect with my Father God. It's a world of absurdity spinning around in my head. These thoughts distract me from being in God's presence and allowing him to speak to my heart.

This distraction not only occurs in church—it pervades my life. It's there from the moment I wake up and don't have time for Bible study because I have to check email, to the moments before bed when I pick up my *Real Simple* magazine or get sucked into bad cable TV. During the day, things like phone calls from friends and work appointments take priority over spending five minutes with my Lord who gave me all of these things. I find myself saying, "I know, God, I need to sit down and pray, but I'm so busy right now and I'll do it in a minute."

I've noticed that when I get up and plan my day, it's not like I ask God's opinion about it. No, I'm perfectly content to tackle the world all by myself. How bad is that? Are we ever really that busy? No! I can't figure it out ... why are Lifetime television movies so much more appealing than reading the Bible? I get sucked in every time. I mean, Victoria Principal is a talented actress, but come on! How many times can I watch her kids get stolen by her ex-husband?

I find that the distractions come each time I want to ask God to light the fire in my heart again, like David prays in Psalm 51:12: "Restore to me the joy of your salvation and grant me a willing spirit, to sustain me." God will always take me back; he's unlike any man on this earth. We can stray from him to other lovers, money, career, stress, worldly possessions, even ministries, but he is patiently waiting with his arms open wide, inviting us back to the greatest love affair we could ever imagine. I want to go there again. How about you?

16

being a cool catholic

Catholics were the coolest when I was growing up. My dad and his whole family are Irish and Italian Catholics. It didn't make me sound zealous or fanatical to say I was Catholic. It was cool and most of my friends went to (and slept through) Mass with their families just like I did. I couldn't stay awake. And when I was awake I spent a lot of my time jabbing my dad who would be nodding off. I'm thankful it was only forty-five minutes; then we were off to the buffet or something more stimulating.

In the seventh grade we had to go through the Sacrament of Confirmation. It's the equivalent of a Bat Mitzvah, if I were a Jewish girl, but without reciting from the Torah. The parties are much smaller and you receive less cash. But still, it was tradition. We'd have to go to these special—and boring—classes on Wednesday nights to prepare to be "confirmed" and accepted as adult members of the church. Thinking back, it's not like we were forced to really see the meaning behind this ceremony; otherwise, I'm sure it would have been more interesting. But at thirteen, the only thing I was interested in was who was on the cover of the *Teen Beat* magazine that I'd smuggle into class. My heart was far from God.

Confirmation is kind of a Catholic "coming out" party. The big thing we had to do was choose a saint whose name we adopted as our confirmation name. The bishop would come to our church and one by one he would bless us and call us by our saint's name in front of all our loved ones. Afterward, we had our party.

Choosing a saint's name was supposed to be a thoughtful decision, but everyone knew all the girls would choose Mary and all the guys would choose John. Well, my friend Kathy and I decided we would be different. As I was reading an article on my crush of the month, Corey Haim (*License to Drive* and *The Lost Boys*), I was reminded of his classic film *Lucas*. There it was—my saint's name. Hey, no one told me any guidelines regarding gender. I would be a revolutionary, I thought. Kathy also chose a nontraditional confirmation name—Zoe.

See, here's the deal ... no one saw our choice of saint until the actual confirmation ceremony. At that time we were to write it on a card and present it to the bishop when it was our turn in line. So when it came time for the ceremony, I was in line with all the other kids in the front of the cathedral as the St. Marys, Michaels, and Johns were being announced. Then it was my turn. The bishop took my card and with a brief hesitation said something like, "I now confirm you, St. Kerri Lucas Pomarolli!" It didn't get the rave reviews I had hoped for. Actually, I think my parents were in shock; they didn't know whether to pray for me or kill me. They laugh about it now, and so do I. I guess I didn't take those rituals too seriously at the time. And hey, stage time is stage time. Why not go for the attention?

What an idiot I was! I'm not proud of that incident. I realize that I never bought into the theory that rituals would bring me any closer to God. I see their beauty now, but the Catholic teachings of my youth relied on the rituals too much. My teachers didn't teach me of a loving Father I could pray to in my bedroom, a gracious God who wants to hear about my successes and failures. I did learn about the fear of the Lord, but even that seemed so distant; God seemed to be so vague and so far away. That's not the God I know now. My parents did a good job of teaching me about God's love though. I don't remember denominations really meaning much in my family. Mom is a Presbyterian and they just taught me to love God and his Son, Jesus.

Let me say this before I go on: I have met some amazing Spirit-filled Catholics in my life. I know now it's not about the denomination; it's about where your heart is when you're there. I didn't open my heart to God's teachings until I was out of college, found a pastor I understood, and stayed awake during his sermons. It could have easily been a priest but that was just not the plan. I do miss the bingo though.

When people ask me what kind of church I attend, I just say, "Christian — and it's really fun." And I actually mean it!

17

me, me, me, and more me

Do you ever stop and think about who or what occupies most of your thoughts? Is it God? Is it your stressful job? Or maybe that cute guy you have been flirting with? It finally dawned on me that most of my prayers revolve around pleasing me! I'm very selfish and want to have more of a servant's heart, but I realized that from the time I get up in the morning until I go to bed, I do only what's comfortable for me. I don't want to get out of my comfort zone. I spend my days and prayers finding ways to make my life easier and more comfortable just like the commercials advertise. The media has made a killing selling products and books and organizers that will make life "easier." Believe me, I've bought them all and I'm still buyin'!

I knew I wanted to read the Bible and spend some time with God yesterday morning and that I didn't have to leave my apartment until noon. At nine o'clock I got dressed and ready, glanced at the Bible on my bed, but decided to step into my office just for a minute to make some calls ... which led to answering email ... which led to paying bills ... which led to a whole financial analysis of the last month with my bank. I kept thinking about praying and reading, but things like cleaning my kitchen seemed more pressing ... and all along I continued to play on my trusty friend, the computer, sending out emails, which I deemed important. Email has been such a vice in my life. Don't laugh; some people have addictive personalities. Email is that instant communication that I love, but I need to keep it under control because it sucks hours out of my day.

When I finally went to pray, guess what? It was noon, and I was stressed and running out the door. My day could have started so much better, but I let the world take over and gave God a backseat. Why? I don't know ... but at least I'm becoming more aware of it. Today when I awoke, I found some time to read his Word and I feel so much calmer. I'm just glad God is never too busy to spend time with me.

18

love me!
validate me!

I'd like to tell you about what my parents affectionately call "The Mac Years." If there were ever two years that I could apologize to my parents for and then remove from everyone's memory, it would be my junior and senior years in high school.

By that time I had established myself as quite the social butterfly and matchmaker. This role kept me in the middle of things; I could overcome my fear of being left out of events by planning them. This fear was with me all through grade school. Really! I would dread recess because I was so terrified I wouldn't have anyone to play with. It didn't help matters that my school was tiny and there were only three girls in the whole third grade class. I always ended up playing ball with the boys just to feel accepted.

It's funny how our childhood fears can stay with us well into adulthood. I became the organizer of weekend events in the small midwestern town where I went to high school. When the homecoming dance came around, my phone was ringing off the hook with calls from guys wanting a date. Not with me, of course—with one of my lovely friends. They weren't even that picky. One guy called me with two choices. We weighed the pros and cons and came to an intelligent decision—he would go with bachelorette A. This girl happened to be my best friend. She was a nice girl with long-term girlfriend potential. To make a long story short, he took my advice and ended up marrying her!

Well, I took matters into my own hands—big surprise—and set myself up with the new kid from Wisconsin. He was shy, sweet, and quiet. Mac had all the makings of a great boyfriend ... looks, a family car on weekends, a letter jacket from football, and the ability to be the most adoring boy on the face of the earth. I called it adoring; my friends called it annoying, and his friends called it "whipped." I often thought he should wear a T-shirt that said, "I can lift heavy objects." You get the picture, right?

At football practice his friends would say, "So what do you have planned this weekend, Mac? Maybe some yard work over at the Pomarollis'?" They were relentless. He just shook his head and never fought back. And the tormenting was even worse because we hadn't "sealed the deal," as they called it. Some girlfriends even let their boyfriends lie about it to save face, but I found that appalling. I was a crusader for righteousness and purity, and in the process, made football practice a living nightmare for my boyfriend. Oh yeah, Mac could bench press 320 pounds and I was pretty proud of that too.

Okay, again you ask, "What's your point?" I knew Mac was the perfect "Mr. Right Now"; he managed to meet all of my needs. He would write me notes every day, telling me how wonderful I was and all the reasons he was glad I came into his life. One time he wrote "I ♥ you" on every line of a piece of paper—both sides! Is that love ... or insanity? I'll take it!

I would profess my undying affection for him as well, and we would gross everyone out by hanging all over each other in the hallways at school and at my house. My poor parents! I can imagine their dismay at my utterly disgusting behavior. There's no other word for it. It was just that Mac made me feel unconditionally accepted, cared for, admired, and most of all, pretty. I became too dependent on him for my self-esteem. I found myself saying things that were out of character for me just to please him and to ensure he stuck around.

Of course, you would think this was enough validation. By this time I had what Mac called "my backup list," which was a list of all my ex-boyfriends and guy friends. Whenever Mac and I would get in a fight, I would call them and they would tell me I was pretty and that he was a loser. Not to mention my father, who was convinced that every man on the planet—gay or straight—was in love with his daughter.

So why the need for "more" all of the time? Was I addicted to attention? Is that why I love acting so much, or do all little girls crave that much love and adoration? It wasn't healthy. If Mac and I were fighting, my whole world would crumble. So many tears were shed, and to this day I can't even remember what we fought about. I'd call Todd in Missouri, and he would promise to buy me that island and marry me someday. Well, at least I had that part of my life locked in. Like I said, I'm a planner.

I never experienced that peace of feeling completely, 100 percent loved. Know why? Because no man can ever give that to me—only God can. If I could have learned that at sixteen, I don't know how much heartache I could have saved myself and those around me. I'm told I was quite the drama queen. There are stories about me throwing a red shoe at Mac after a dance because he wouldn't get out of the car until the football game was over on the radio. I have faint memories of "After School Special" moments where I come home crying my eyes out to my dad and he tells me to "just buck up and remember that these are Mac's glory days."

All these nostalgic memories are flooding my brain because I'll be seeing him with his new wife next month at my high school reunion. Alas, another one bites the dust and gets happily married. I never even considered marrying Mac. As far as I was concerned in high school, he was my ticket to popularity and validation until I moved on to bigger and better things, like college boys. I guess we learn something from every relationship.

Those years taught me a lot. I learned that men will break your heart and that kisses aren't contracts. But if I had trusted in God instead of my own emotions back then, I wouldn't have suffered half as much as I did. I just didn't know enough to turn it over to God. I didn't think he cared about the small stuff, but we all know he did and still does. I still don't understand Christian dating and all this "courting stuff." Did God not want me to have a boyfriend in high school? Was I supposed to be home alone playing Yahtzee while all my friends were out at football games and dances falling in and out of love? I really don't know.

I pray to him about guys all the time now, especially when one rejects me and I get frustrated. I just say, "Okay Lord, I get it ... not the one for me ... moving on," and I drive home. Of course, I now complain to him the whole way, but it's progress.

19

italy

One summer in high school I went off to Italy with my good friend Kelly to do a play. We had so many adventures. And, for the record, all of them were sober. Well, at least mine were. We were on a tour doing an operetta called *The Bacchae.* Kelly and I were by far the youngest members of the troupe. Everyone thought we were being supervised by everyone else, so we were basically on our own.

I was leaving my boyfriend, Mac, back at home, and I was distraught over this—for about forty-eight hours. I actually had my first panic attack on the airplane to Italy—no joke! Was I stressed about being in a foreign country? No! I just didn't want to leave my boyfriend. They actually had to rush me off the airplane from the runway to the emergency room, only to find out I was not having a heart attack but was just nervous. Well, twenty-four hours and two Zanax later, I was back on the plane to Italy … only after a lot of coaxing from my father who had already paid for my trip!

I quickly got over it when Kelly and I met Antonio, Andre, Sebastian, Marco, and some of the locals, whose English consisted of the phrases "I love you" and "marry me." It was pure bliss. They got a kick out of Americans, and we were glad to be Americans for them. It was instant validation times ten! They thought we were rich, that we would marry them and take them back to our country. I think I told one guy my dad owned Ford Motor Company. We flirted our little hearts out and fell in love ten times a week. Kelly found particular fame one night singing the National Anthem while standing on a bistro table.

Ahhh, to be young and naïve again. It was all so innocent, but it backs up my principle that we women just want to be validated. Kelly and I were shameless with our big hair and little dresses. Besides, my friends Suzy and Liz back home decided it wasn't officially cheating on Mac if it was outside the continental United States. So there you go. I was seventeen at the time and that logic made perfect sense. What happens in Italy ... stays in Italy.

While others on our tour were looking at great museums, Kelly and I were studying the finer culture ... like the Benetton clothing store and how many men would propose to us that day. One weekend we snuck off to Florence and went dancing. At the end of the night we met two Canadians, Rob and Adam.

At that point we were happy to meet anyone who didn't speak broken English. To be honest, we were kind of freaked out to be in the big city alone. Rob and Adam were older — nineteen — and pre-med students. College boys! Does "pre-med" even mean anything except that it sounds cool to high school chicks? We were in — hook, line, and sinker. We spent a romantic night roaming the streets of Florence and ended up sleeping on a cardboard box in a park because we couldn't find the *albergo* (hotel) where Kelly and I were staying.

Adam used some classic lines as we sat on a cardboard box in a park at 3:00 a.m.:

Kerri: "But Adam, I can't kiss you. I have a boyfriend." (Long pause, dramatic stare.)

Adam: "Kerri, don't you think it's time for a serious college relationship?" (Dramatic pause ... music starts ... they embrace ... fade to black.)

Magic, I tell you — they can't write this stuff any better! These two guys were so good, we couldn't see straight. We said our dramatic goodbyes and made plans to see our Canadian beaus when we got home. After we parted, Kelly and I immediately wrote them love letters, professing our undying affection.

When we arrived home we arranged for them to visit my house in Michigan for a few days. Kelly's mom drove us to meet Rob and Adam at the Canadian bridge. Adam had this full-on-beard—a new addition—and somehow without the romantic lighting of Italy at one in the morning, he didn't look so appealing. And come to think of it, they both were kind of obnoxious in the car ride home.

My mom had made a pork roast for dinner—which is so *not* kosher (nice, Barb!). Even so, these "nice" Jewish boys had dinner with my family. It was obvious to everyone at the table that Rob and Adam weren't so charming after all; they were talking about all the girls they had met ... right in front of us. My dad especially was *not* impressed. They did not know who they were dealing with. According to my father there were no other girls ... anywhere ... ever! My dad cordially cut their trip short and offered/suggested that he drop them off at their cars at the Canadian bridge the next day. Leave it to Dad to save the day! I still owe him for that one. Okay—live and learn; I was only seventeen. So what's my excuse now?

20

the in crowd

After that summer in Italy, my ego was as big as Texas and there was not a man on earth who was good enough. All the Italians had filled my head with grandeur and fantasy about being so perfect and beautiful. Poor Mac didn't stand a chance. I was beyond annoying and he knew it. I was a diva with a capital *D*. Looking back at the pictures from the Italy trip, I don't see how that could have been possible with that horrific perm I was sporting.

Mac tried to please me at first, but got over it and then tried to break up with me one night at a party. Before I arrived he told people what he was going to do. It was like a scene from *90210* … when I walked in, everyone got quiet and there was a sense of drama in the room. I'm convinced several girls there were excited to see me get dumped. He was waiting for me in the basement. I remember this one girl, Diane, giggling in that Dr. Evil tone from *Austin Powers*. In my clique, everyone was trying to bring everyone else down. It was a battle at all times.

It took a lot of tears and three hours of convincing, but I emerged victorious—relationship with Mac intact. I had to pull out all the stops, but I wasn't about to start my senior year of high school alone. That was a fate worse than death in my book! If I could only go back and do it over, I would have let the other girls have him. We weren't compatible anyway. He was just a security blanket with big muscles in a letter jacket.

School started and Mac and I were together, but I was miserable; now the shoe was on the other foot and Mac was in control. He made me pay for my behavior, and I spent a lot of time making sure he was happy. We had both changed and grown apart from each other, but I was determined to hold on to him until school was over — mainly for social events like homecoming and prom, not to mention the guy/girl pompom routine where you had to have a good looking jock for a partner or you were exiled from "popularity land" forever. The blue sequin prom dresses and pink Lee Press-On Nails — how I miss those days!

I would do whatever it took to be in the "in crowd." I avoided the drinking and drugs; they weren't very prevalent anyway. No one really slept around, and I had the "good girls" as my friends, so that was cool. We all used to be "good girls" before things split. I don't know when it happened. Junior year we were all going to carnivals and movies in huge groups and then senior year some of the girls thought it would be cool to be wild and drink "cranka," their name for cranberry juice mixed with the vodka they stole from their parents' basements. These girls segregated themselves from the rest of us and latched on to any football player they could. Since I was dating one, I had to watch my back at all times. This was a full-time job. I knew a couple girls wanted to steal my boyfriend, and I wasn't about to let that happen without a fight.

I know, we were such godly young women. But I stressed over really important things like sitting at the right lunch table. We'd all race down the ramp to the cafeteria and cram three girls to a chair at the "cool table" — or so we thought. Unbelievable! Were those seats any better? No, but it was at the other end of the table where the guys who all shared one testosterone-filled brain sat. Who wouldn't want to be near that?

Looking back, we were all just a bunch of insecure kids trying to be accepted. Whether it was our trendy Mustang GT's, Ford Probes in Tic Tac green, or the clothes with the labels prominently displayed on the front — it was all a big game. I hated it, but was too scared to *not* play; I didn't think there was a choice. I wanted to have the "quintessential high school experience." That is why I did half the things I did ... because I thought that was what I was supposed to be doing. I think I had watched too many TV shows by that point about what high school was supposed to be. I remember crying a lot ... over what, I don't know, but there always seemed to be some drama bigger than life that sent me into a whirlwind of agony much to my mother's dismay. She had to live with me. And God bless friends like Susie Koster. We would lament for hours about our plans and hopes and dreams after high school. We both had steady boyfriends and knew we had to fight to keep them even though we didn't use sex as a tool, unlike some of our acquaintances. And I'm sure glad about that because everyone knew everything about everybody. Nothing went unnoticed, and looking back I had way too much information about my classmates' sexual escapades in high school. Any guy who says "I won't tell anyone" is lying. Trust me.

Another classmate, Angie, was a sweet, beautiful girl who was our high school class president. She lives in California now too, and we had dinner together last week. She didn't hang with the "cool" crowd in high school. I asked if she dealt with all those insecurities from trying to fit in as I did. For the most part, she didn't. She was smart; she could see even back then how little all that popularity stuff mattered. She said she had a great high school experience. I did too, but it was the best when I felt I was being accepted by everyone. It was hard work trying to be liked all the time. And I never really felt satisfied. I never felt at peace. It was a full-time job worrying about what everybody else was thinking. I wish I would have been more like Angie and seen things for what they really were.

21

what i did for love
or college frat boys

During my college years at the University of Michigan there were many experiences and adventures. None were spiritual, so I'll spare you most of the details. Those years were filled with finding out about who I was ... or so I thought. When I look back at my behavior and thoughts from my journals, I'm embarrassed at how cocky I was. I thought I had it all figured out: cute boys + popular sorority + lots of friends + parties + stretch pants + fabulous "big hair" + more cute boys = success.

Yeah, there were classes and teachers, but for me, those were unimportant details compared to sorority life and what theme party I would be attending that weekend. For the most part my relationship with God was pretty nonexistent. I did have my moments though — I visited a Campus Crusade for Christ meeting and stood in the back because I thought I was too cool to be there. They were all singing and clapping; honestly, it freaked me out. I had never seen anything like that.

I was in a Bible study and even went to a Christian conference once, but that was because it was in Missouri and Todd Kramer was meeting me there. Enough said! I remember getting all emotional over God during that weekend and even crying because I had heard a powerful female speaker, but that's all I recall. I don't remember her message, but it was something about giving your life to God. I do remember wanting to have that personal relationship with God like the others around me at that weekend conference, but it seemed so intangible. The details are totally fuzzy, but God was planting seeds in my life, trying to get my full attention. I realize I was nowhere close to giving it to him. I had my "moment" and then it was over.

There were way too many "loves of my life" to talk about them all, but several need to be mentioned because they inspired some of my all-time greatest do-it-yourself moments. There was Doug Kligman. What can I say? Well, I could mention that women in my sorority would say, "Can we please have a moment of silence for Doug Kligman's abs?" Let me tell you, he had an awesome six-pack, sparkling green eyes, and a smile that was devilishly charming. He could have been the guy on the Pepsodent commercials. He ran for student leadership by posting pictures of himself and his puppy all over campus. I believe he won.

We met one night on the dance floor at the illustrious Sigma Nu fraternity house. No words were spoken; Prince said it all and then so did Marvin Gaye. We had an instant connection and danced until 2:00 a.m. We were the last ones on the dance floor and didn't even care. And even though my Alpha Phi house was about a hundred feet away, and it was a freezing cold Michigan winter night, I asked him to walk me home in the snow. That was code for "Can we go make out at my doorstep?" We didn't make out; we ended up singing 80s love songs well into the night—Journey, REO Speedwagon, etc. We were loud. And believe it or not, we were sober. I knew I had found a soul mate of sorts. I mean, when you find a guy who's straight and good looking and knows all the words to "Love Bites" by Def Leopard, you gotta hold on to him! Can you just picture the two of us outside in the freezing wind belting out at the top of our lungs, "Here with meee!" It brings tears to my eyes just thinking about it.

A few days later I received a call from Doug inviting me on

a "study date" to the grad library. Sounds simple, right? Sure, if I wasn't a musical theater major. See, (a) I had never been to the grad library and didn't even know where it was, and (b) I didn't have any books that didn't have musical notes in them. I am sad to admit this, but I didn't even know how to type at that time. I had to pay my roommate Sarah to type my papers!

So I had to run around my house gathering books for my book bag from my friends. It was hard for them not to laugh hysterically at the thought of me going to the grad library. I just wanted to look studious. I knew we wouldn't study much, but I knew the drill. Anyway, that was his excuse to ask me out. We'd probably get there, sit down, chat, and flirt for half an hour, then leave to get coffee, talk, fall in love, and start a meaningful relationship that would at least last until spring. It was perfect. I'd have a date for the spring formal and be the envy of all my friends. Of course, I had a plan. I *always* had a plan.

So we were off to our study date. We walked into this massive library and the silence was almost scary; I didn't know what to do. I followed Doug around the tables, but there were no cozy corner spots available like I'd planned. Instead, I found myself standing in this tiny cubicle that was encased by high wooden walls. I was thinking, *What are we doing here?* when Doug said, "Okay, here ya go. I'll be back in a few hours." And then he was gone. *What?* I was in total disbelief. This was not at all how I pictured our evening. And there I was sitting in this cubicle — *alone* — with nothing to do. I resorted to whittling my initials in the desk and writing notes to my friends like a seventh grader. I stuck it out though and was bored out of my mind. I think if it was today, I wouldn't have waited ten minutes for a guy in a cubicle, so maybe I've matured at least a little. Or maybe I'm just more of a diva?

Anyway, we did end up going for coffee like I had predicted, and thus began my beautiful relationship with Doug Kligman that has been through many seasons. Doug and I soon realized that we were best suited as soul mates on the friendship level. We were both in college to enjoy it to the fullest and commitment wasn't in our vocabulary, but we had such a great time together that we had to figure out a way to stay in each other's radar. I think we knew that each of us was headed for an interesting journey, and we wanted to see how it all played out.

Boyfriends come and go but some friendships last a lifetime. We started out on the dance floor in Ann Arbor and then he moved to LA to go to law school, and we saw each other through many breakups and makeups. The best thing was that Doug and I were so similar; we knew exactly how to communicate with each other. Our motto was and still is, "Flattery will get you everywhere!" He is now officially my number one male confidant and personal advocate. I can call him up day or night, and he'll immediately tell me how perfect and beautiful I am in every way, sparing no detail. Gotta love men like that. Doug always tells me I'm like a fine wine ... I get better with age. He even manages to say it with a totally straight face, and I love him for it.

22

lee press-on nails and tales from the bus stop

I've been through a really tough month health-wise. I've had all these tests and the doctors are unable to figure out where this pain is coming from. I keep trying to have a positive attitude because that is what I want the people in my life to see. People are always telling me I'm "so strong" and that I "inspire them." I don't want to let anyone down. But I don't feel strong—I'm scared and don't like what the doctors tell me when they call.

This sickness has really kept me down—physically and, at times, emotionally. As I write this, I'm on a plane to attend my high school reunion. I was advised not to go, but I decided I wouldn't give in to feeling bad; I really want to be there. My date for the reunion is Doug Kligman, the hot guy who left me in the library in college. He'll look good in pictures and besides, we'll have a blast. We're great friends now, but I'm still nervous.

So I made all the necessary preparations for a class reunion. I brought my black sequined pantsuit—very LA. I had to wear sequins—it's a trademark and my friends would expect nothing less. I'd skip the blue eye shadow and Lee Press-On Nails that went over so well at my prom, but I got my hair cut and styled and even applied my self-tanner for that "all-natural" California look. And don't forget the manicure and pedicure. How insecure am I? I'm turning into my mother! Yikes!

It takes me back to the first day of public school in eighth grade in my new town. I had accidentally — on purpose — dyed my hair a unique shade of pink with the help of my pal Jen Johnson and that stuff called Zazu. My mom got so mad and told me to fix it, so I snuck into my grandpa's bathroom and poured peroxide on my head for a lovely tri-dye effect. It was so natural! And if that wasn't enough, I had these pink Lee Press-On Nails — cotton-candy pink — to match the shimmering pink lipstick and blue eyeliner that was supposed to match my eyes. It all went perfectly with my new denim skirt and pink blouse. Hey, it was the 80s, okay?

I had never ridden a bus to school before eighth grade. I showed up at the bus stop, got on, and managed to make it back to the bus at the end of the day. Public school was a blur compared to the small Christian school I came from where my seventh grade class had only five kids. Who would have thought opening a locker could be so difficult? But more important, it was a sea of new faces — new, good looking, eighth-grade boy faces. In particular, all the girls were talking about Ryan Robison and his new haircut. And guess what? He rode *my* bus! He was so cute in that spiked-hair kinda way.

So I'm sitting in a seat across from him, talking to a nice girl named Sandy who lived on my street. All of a sudden one of my Lee Press-On Glamour Nails popped off and fell onto the bus floor. There it was, shining up at me. I didn't dare move to pick it up and reveal my secret. I was frozen. Well, what do you think happened? Ryan reached down, quietly picked it up, and asked who it belonged to. My neighbor, Kimi, loudly announced, "It's Kerri's Lee Press-On Nail!" If the window had been bigger, I would have jumped. I survived that moment and managed not to kill Kimi with my bare hands. Ryan went on to become my science lab partner, good pal, and that same guy who ended up marrying my best friend. Go figure!

What's my point? Well, it's years later, and I'm still worried about my nails! Old habits die hard. I just had to have my California hair, California tan, and my California life. You know what's so ironic? I've been working out and working out to look thin for this weekend, and this dumb illness has made my stomach swell up to where I look mildly pregnant. Classic ... just classic.

It occurred to me today as I was driving my car and lamenting over my appearance: God thinks I'm beautiful—not just okay-looking—but really beautiful just the way he made me. He doesn't even care about how my hair looks or if my face breaks out. He cares about the woman I am from the inside out. I've heard this before and always thought it sounded cheesy, but I think I get it now. He loves me so unconditionally and is so proud of the woman I've become in him. I can just imagine him up there saying, "I think you're beautiful, Kerri, and I will never leave you. Just go and have fun this weekend." I'm going to try my best to keep this in my heart when I run into ex-boyfriends and friends from my past, because in God, my past is forgotten. I'm also going to try my best to remember this when I feel totally single and have to spend the evening looking at engagement rings and baby pictures, hearing about new homes and "grown-up" things that my classmates are doing. I'll just smile and say, "That's great for you! I can hardly keep my plants alive and my idea of 'grown-up' these days is being home before *Saturday Night Live*."

Isaiah 43:18–19 says, "Forget the former things; do not dwell on the past. See, I am doing a new thing!" That's me; I'm a new creature because of Christ's love. He died so I could be born again, and no one can take that away from me. No one can make me feel less than worthy of everything God desires for me.

I'm sure that my life isn't what my friends expected it to be—after all, I was voted "Most Likely to Get Married in Las Vegas Several Times." But my life is better than I ever expected it to be. God never ceases to amaze me. No, I don't have my own TV series or my beach house yet, but I have a Savior who loves me and watches over me and will never let me fall. What more could a girl ask for? Okay, okay ... don't get me started.

The reunion ended up being fun and mostly anticlimactic. All the people I hung out with basically looked the same as I remembered, and we ended up just sitting around talking like no time had passed. There were no dramatic moments—just a lot of polite greetings like, "You look so great" and "What are you up to now?" It was fine. My ex, Mac, was not there but that's okay. Doug and I had a blast, and it was worth the trip to see people and to catch up.

One of my favorite moments was when a guy from my class, who shall remain nameless, came up to me at the end of the night. Let's just say he was mildly drunk. He said in a really long, slurred sentence, "So Kerri, do you ah ... like ... want to have kids?" "Yeah, I do," I answered, smiling as I tried to avoid his beer breath, and as he was invading my personal space. "No! I mean like now ... tonight with me!" "Wow! That is such a tempting offer, but I think I have to go now. Thanks for asking, and I'll see you in ten years!" Some things never change.

My health held up amazingly well. Right after I returned home to California, the doctors found out what had made me so sick—I had contracted a parasite. Within just a few days of being on antibiotics, I was totally well. I have to look back on those couple months of uncertainty as times where I had no choice but to totally cry out to God. I felt really close to him and dependent on him. If I could just master that type of closeness with him when I'm well ... that would be cool.

23

mortified

I'm doing a show called "Mortified," and it's about several comedians reading totally uncensored excerpts from their teenage diaries. As you know, I've been keeping diaries off and on since the third grade. So lately I've had the chance to read them and relive some of the great love affairs of my life. It's been crazy looking back. I can read from 1991 and then 1998 and then 2003 and they still sound the same in some ways. We definitely develop relationship patterns; mine is trying to emulate a great romance movie. So I either fall for the incredibly handsome bad boy—the one I can't get—or the sweet, sensitive, hopeless romantic. But without fail, 99 percent of these relationships start out like some AMC classic movie and end with a sad, strong dose of reality TV. Me alone with my chocolate chip cookies and all my friends telling me he wasn't good enough for me. Maybe I'm not so different from all the other little girls growing up and dreaming of being swept off their feet. I think I was just a little more proactive about achieving this goal.

You already know about my first love, Todd Kramer. We kept that fantasy going for many years, seeing each other occasionally and reigniting that passionate bond that formed in a video arcade in Boston at the Ford Auto Show. We both wanted the fairy tale, and one day we met up and talked face-to-face about a real future. We realized we had grown up exactly as we thought—he a successful car dealer in Missouri, taking over his family's business, playing with his boats and airplanes, and me out in Los Angeles pursuing my acting dream. We didn't really love each other enough to leave our lives and dreams behind for the other. It was bittersweet that day because I knew it would never be the same between us and we had grown up and out of our fantasy. It's okay now—he's happily married to a beautiful model, no less, and he will always hold a special place in my heart. However, he wasn't really a practicing Christian, and God knew he wasn't what I needed—even though what Todd had to offer me was very tempting and it would have been a nice life in Missouri! He would have taken very good care of me, and I'm sure he's a wonderful husband. Yikes! Husband. Wow, that sounds so grown-up.

24

jewish love – los angeles style

This memoir would not be complete without the mention of my very first Jewish love in Los Angeles. It was my first long-term, out of college "grown-up" relationship, and I learned a lot from acting like a total teenager for two whole years. Let's call him "Steve," since he's into politics now and being in a Christian "tell all" would be scandalous for him!

Well, my relationship with Steve was quite a ride. He was a good midwestern boy who moved to California to start his own business. We met watching a Michigan football game at eight o'clock at some bar in Westwood. He was so adorable and had a smile that told you he was always up to something. He ran his own businesses since he was a teen and was very successful at whatever he chose to pursue. I'm sure he'll end up on the cover of *Newsweek* someday. He's just that smart. He was goofy, fun, sweet, romantic, and success-driven (which is the quality I was most attracted to).

Everyone always told us how cute we were together. He was about 5' 7"; I'm 5' 2". Steve didn't live in my city, so we spent long weekends together and many late nights on the phone. He was everything I'd ever wanted: He was successful, had good values, and treated me really well—romantic dinners, surprise outings to the theater, and long drives in the mountains. You name it, he did it. It was the fairy tale, but this time I was out in California with no rules and no parents and the sky was the limit on what might happen.

We fell head-over-heels in love with each other by about our second date. I don't ever remember being more giddy over a guy. I had just arrived in California, and Steve was everything I ever dreamed of. I was being swept off my feet. We had so much in common it was scary, and we immediately assumed the role of official "soul mates." I was his second serious girlfriend, and he told me things that melted my heart. Within three weeks we had pledged our undying love and affection for one another. Of course, the subject of religion never came up. I just thought that little detail would work itself out.

Those times were exciting, fun, and blissful for us. I finally thought I had arrived. I was living in Los Angeles, following my dreams, and had this amazing confidant, boyfriend, cheerleader, and partner in Steve. We were almost a comedy act. People would love to watch us interact because it was always entertaining, especially when we fought. When we bickered, our timing would rival that of any vaudeville act.

What I didn't see was that we were both type-A personalities —dominant, controlling, and sarcastic. And we loved to ride that emotional roller coaster all the way to the top and drop down again at a moment's notice. If I had recorded some of our exchanges at that time, I'm sure I could have sold them to MTV as the basis for some teen drama/comedy.

Like me, Steve had an intense personality, so after six months or so, the friendly bickering escalated to fighting. When we fought, we fought! We were kicked out of movie theaters for throwing Slurpees on one another. We went on a game show together and did crazy stunts for cash and prizes. We almost didn't make it on the show because we nearly killed each other in the dressing room. There was no middle ground; we were either way up or way down.

I believe I was so addicted to Steve because we didn't know to set any boundaries in the relationship. We just jumped in and gave each other 110 percent from the get-go—emotionally and even physically, to some degree. This was back before I was the "nun" I am now! Of course, we were going to be blinded to any problems—we were too busy being passionate. Toward the end of our almost two-year relationship, he even said to me, "Kerri, with us it's either passion or carnage." Now that I think of it, I'm sure our problems were due to being young and immature. After we were together for a year, I wrote in my journals that I knew this could never work, but I couldn't find the strength to leave. We had become so intertwined in each other's lives, it would be like cutting off my right arm. I prayed to God to help me get out of the relationship, but there was always some stupid excuse I had in my head for not breaking up with him—my birthday was coming ... or some major holiday—you know, the really important reasons for staying together.

The religious differences did surface after awhile, and there was no compromise from either of us. It's not like he was a religious Jew at all. In fact, he was an atheist, but culturally he wanted to marry someone Jewish even though he never intended to practice. He did his best to pull me out of any religious beliefs I had.

I attended church alone and he called me a religious zealot. I prayed and prayed for God to change his heart, but he never budged—not even a little. I had a relationship with God, but I was still ignoring his guidance for my life. I felt convicted about being in this relationship, but not to the point where I could take a stand.

Through all the drama we stayed together. I went to Hawaii with my family toward the very end of our relationship, and this *hot* valet from our hotel took me on a tour of the island. Ladies, I kid you not ... when I saw him take off his shirt and dive into the ocean, my jaw visibly dropped. It was like an episode of *Baywatch* where the waves are crashing and everything seems to be in slow motion. He was a nationally ranked surfer, and I think he's one of the guys you see on "Hot in Hawaii" posters.

After a romantic swim in the ocean, he asked me to meet up with him that evening. I was ready to go hang out with him and his friends, and then I thought of Steve back home. I couldn't go. Can you believe it? I could have hit myself. When I got home and Steve and I were in some huge fight, I pulled out that whole story just to make him feel bad. Steve just laughed and said, "You should have gone. I would have."

We broke up shortly after Hawaii. Painful does not even begin to describe how the breakup felt. Steve was my ultimate validation; almost every day he would tell me in ten different ways how beautiful and amazing and smart I was. But we knew we weren't a match for the long-term — not only because of our religious differences, but because we drove each other mad most of the time. It's not worth reevaluating why it didn't work; it just didn't, and we finally moved on from each other. But it was painful!

Steve is now a multimillionaire and engaged to a wonderful girl. We have remained friends, but he still bugs me at times. It's not like I moved on right away; it took at least three weeks.

25

moving on —
an officer and a lady

Okay, so I'm either a fast healer or incredibly needy — you choose. That next summer I was literally swept off my feet again by a handsome young Marine named Rick. I was at our local beach bar with my girlfriends and this guy had moves I had never seen before. He approached me and introduced himself. When he found out I was a nice Catholic girl who went to the University of Michigan, he invited me to the Notre Dame versus Michigan football game that coming fall at Notre Dame, his alma mater in Indiana. "Funny," I said. He meant it.

Rick gave me every line, telling me this was destiny, he and I. He wanted my phone number and I refused. So as he said later, he "put his hard hat on and went to work." He told me he was a nice Catholic boy from Colorado (10+) and gave half his Las Vegas winnings to the church (another 10+). He even sang "You've Lost That Lovin' Feelin'" while on his knees right there in the bar with his roommate/sidekick. You could tell they had this rehearsed. I think they also threw in a Bon Jovi love ballad, harmony and all.

Finally, I mentioned I was tired, but there was no place to sit. He went up to these guys at another table and bought them a round of drinks so they would move and I could have a place to sit. He said,

"Have you ever kissed a guy in a bar?" "No," I said. "Well, you're not going to start now!" He was good! I was in—hook, line, and sinker. I gave him my phone number on a napkin and floated all the way home. I mean, he was a Christian—he even said it. This was a first for me, and I was all for it. This was obviously God's work. I had been single for three weeks, and it was just so romantic to meet a guy in a bar on the Hermosa Pier, right?

The next three days were the longest of my natural life. I finally got a call from Rick, and we made plans to go to dinner that next weekend. He lived two hours away in San Diego, so we met in the middle and had a wonderful time eating at a place on the beach. The minute I saw him in his green polo shirt and khakis, I was done. He looked so hot in that all-American "I could take this guy home to my father" way. Not to mention, my dad would love that he was a Marine. We laughed, and he was beyond charming.

We were discussing how we met and he leans over and says, "Okay, so you can tell your grandchildren this is how it happened ..." He then proceeded to tell me how he saw me across a crowded room, not missing a detail. The song from *Peter Pan*—"I'm Flying ... Flying"—would best describe the evening. It ended with a sweet hug. After our first date he walked me to the car and slowly leaned in and planted one soft kiss right on my cheek, smiled and said, "See you next week." I'm telling you, this guy was *good*!

We started talking on the phone nightly and seeing each other on the weekends. I went down with my girlfriends and met up with him in San Diego. I remember him introducing me as his girlfriend after two weeks. And as usual, he talked about our future together. He had all these plans for things we were going to do. I bought every line. He told me he had never met anyone like me, never been attracted to anyone like this, and thought I could be "the one." He even gave me flowers. (Okay, he picked them from someone's yard, but he even made *that* seem romantic and charming.) We had the important things in common like 80s music and mint chocolate chip ice cream—you know ... the things that make a relationship work.

Oh, yes! I need to tell you, Mr. Rick was going to be shipped overseas in the fall for six months. Can we say, "Turner Classic Movie" or what? I loved the drama of it all! We didn't talk about it much. When I was in the midst of all this, I truly believed Rick was sincere. Even his roommate told me he had never seen Rick like this before. He said that prior to my visit, Rick had scrubbed the entire apartment top-to-bottom, military style.

I liked his boldness in telling me how he felt and making his intentions clear. He didn't care who was around; he was proud to have me as his companion. He even announced to a bunch of his friends that I would be his date to the Marine Ball that next winter. They all told me they hadn't seen him so into a girl before and that was the best part for me. Can you picture it? Me out on the town with my handsome Marine boyfriend and his charismatic friends giving me added attention? Can we say, *Officer and a Gentleman*? It's just that we were so infatuated with the idea of one another, we took things to warp speed way too soon.

Why am I reporting this stuff to you now? Because looking back at our past relationships, we can see the patterns we develop and hopefully learn from them. No, I never went to the Marine Ball with Mr. Rick; we sort of fizzled out as quickly as we got started. With the two-hour distance and our busy schedules, we just couldn't make it work. Shocker! He had this fantasy I'd move to San Diego, and I thought he would move to Los Angeles.

Okay, to be honest, getting over Rick was harder than any guy I'd ever dated. I kept thinking, *What if he wasn't leaving? What if he really was "the one" that got away?* I drove myself crazy all summer! We talked a couple months later—right before he was leaving for at least six months. It was obvious that we were still not over each other. He sang to me, told me he missed me, and then hung up and shipped out.

I was still heartbroken. I prayed to God to help me get over Rick, but I had no idea I had done this to myself—yet again. Boundaries, Kerri, boundaries! I didn't believe in them. I thought if I gave 100 percent to everything else, why didn't it work that way in love? No one told me anything about guarding my heart. I just gave it away with each new love, hoping to find the one that would stick forever—finally.

About eight months later I got a phone call out of the blue. I was actually on a date at the time and the voice on the other end made the hairs on my arms stand up. It was Rick and he was back. I was speechless because in nine seconds flat he had managed to tug at my heart strings, get my blood pressure up, and ruin my current date with a nice boy from the Coast Guard! He immediately started launching into his monologue of how "he had to see me." He had some important things to talk to me about. He had this presence about him even over the phone that was confident and commanding; I just couldn't say no. He had been thinking of me nonstop on the ship while he was gone. Well, that's a no-brainer. I'm not sure there were any women on that vessel for him to think about other than the ones on cable.

He did the hard sell and I was in. We made plans to meet up the following weekend at the same beach bar where we first met. He would be in town visiting friends, and I would bring some of my girlfriends as backup. I made my friend Jessica a deal before we left for the evening. "Do not let me leave with him to go anywhere. I do not want to be alone with him; no matter what I say, stick by me." That way I wouldn't put myself in any tempting situations and risk getting too emotionally involved again.

So we met up and the chemistry was still there, no doubt. We danced and tried to hold a conversation, but it was a loud Saturday night at Sharkees on the Beach, so it was really hard to hear. At one point he pulled Jessica aside and told her I was the most amazing woman he had ever met. I was all he thought about while he was away. He wanted me back and knew he had screwed things up before. I thought that was a nice touch—trying to win over the friend first—but she wasn't buying it.

After more dancing to romantic classics like Prince, we all decided to go to a house party on the beach. Rick was kind of insinuating that he and I could go somewhere else, but, as planned, I insisted we go to the party as a group. So we arrived and Rick was annoyed. I'm having a great time, and all he wants to do is leave. "Let's go walk on the beach and talk," he said. "We can talk fine right here and besides, we're thirty feet from the beach as it stands. Plus I don't want to leave my friends." "Fine! Be that way," he said in a total Dr. Jekyll moment. His entire demeanor changed. He was really mad that he wasn't getting his way.

He walked off the porch and started to walk away ... I was in shock. "Where are you going?" I asked in that *90210* holding-back-tears voice. "This obviously isn't going to work. You don't even trust me. All I wanted to do was spend some time with you and talk, but your friends are more important." (Cue the music ... dramatic 80s teen movie exit approaching.) "Goodbye, Kerri," and he disappeared into the dark. I stood there in utter disbelief at what had just happened.

I couldn't think; I was just shaking all over. Had that actually just happened? Had Rick walked out of my life as quickly as he walked in? A *second* time? And how had I let him do it? What was wrong with me? How could I have let this happen? I needed closure or therapy—not sure which one.

I ran into the house and told Jess what happened, and she didn't seem too surprised. But in that typical Laverne and Shirley fashion, we didn't want to let this moment die. We had to have a plan. So we went home and found the number of his friend where he was staying, and at 3:00 a.m., with Jess listening in on the other line, I called him. Can you believe it? What an idiot!

He answered ... I was calm. He was near silent. He didn't have anything to say to me, and I didn't have the words to describe my emotions at that point. "Uh, Rick ... are you okay? Is that really the way you want to leave things? You walk into my life and walk right out like that?" His poetic response was, "Kerri, you need someone more mature." "You're absolutely right. Goodbye, Rick." And that was that.

26

changes

Okay, picture it: A late night on the town in Hollywood. My girl-friends have had a few too many martinis and I, being the sober one, am forced to listen to their "I've had too much to drink and now I think I'm hilarious" humor. I am annoyed. I just want to go home, but my cell phone rings. It's my friend Dan asking if we want to meet him and his friend Jake at Swingers, another hipster diner/late-night hangout. Well, maybe a banana split couldn't hurt.

We arrived at Swingers to see Dan and this mysterious stranger sitting in a booth. He was a cross between James Dean and Matthew Perry in looks. He had long hair, a serious suede jacket from the 1960s, and deep blue eyes that were sad in that poetic kind of way. He didn't say much, but when he did, whatever remarks that were made came out with surprising dry wit. I was attracted to that ... very attracted. He had this intensity about him, and I could tell he was watching every move I made. We had communicated without words that it was annoying to both of us how completely blitzed my friends were, and how I was the "sober sis" of the group.

He stepped outside to smoke a cigarette which, in my opinion, is the most disgusting thing a human can do. When he came back in I said loudly enough for the next three tables to hear, "Smoking's *out!*" He smiled slightly and didn't say a word. This guy was sexy, no doubt about it—in that bad-boy-scruffy-untamed way. I heard myself uttering in my mind the words every girl at one point in her life has uttered, "I will change him." It's not like it was a conscious thought. I think it's genetic that immature girls like me want to take the guy who is the most unattainable player and make him hers … mainly to show off to their friends and to say they did it. I loved a challenge, and he was a prime target.

As we left the diner, somewhere around 2:00 a.m., I turned around to hear Jake yelling my name. I came back to the door, and he said, "I thought you could use a hug. It was nice to meet you." He hugged me, and we parted ways. As I floated home, my friends' ranting didn't even bother me. I had plans for me and Mr. Jake—and my mind was full-speed ahead.

Well, the next day came and as I probed my friend Terry for any details about what Jake might have said about me, I found out that Jake said, "She's the kind of girl you take to lunch and then home to Mom." Okay, so this was good … until I found out that Dan had refused to give my number to his friend because he was afraid he would end up hurting me. Whatever! What was this? My big brother talking? I was perfectly capable of making my own decisions, thank you! (Irrational or otherwise.)

So the days and weeks went on, and I made many excuses to be around Terry and his new friend Jake. There were parties where I would follow him around and literally not get out of his face until he put out the "cancer stick" that was in his mouth. I was shameless, and he didn't know what to make of me. Looking back, knowing what I know, it was that he knew I wasn't like the other girls he was used to. I was a "nice girl" and a guy like him had some decisions to make before really committing to dating his new best friend's good friend.

The nights would end in the same way. We would flirt shamelessly, and then I would go home and be more frustrated each time. Whenever I saw him I would find out something more intriguing about his life and his adventures, from boarding school to European travels, to his family, which came from the South like mine. We connected for sure, but it took three months for him to finally steal my cell phone number off Dan's phone and ask me out. I'm so glad he did because I was sick of coming up with hypothetical reasons to coincidentally be in his "neighborhood"—it being a locked, gated community and all.

That first date was lovely. We went to a pub, talked, laughed, and flirted. I thought I was being so deep because there was something about this guy that seemed more intense than the others I had dated. He was quieter and talked of things like world affairs and philosophy. I told him that first night he needed to be "rescued" and I was up for the job. Rescued from what, I didn't know, but I sensed this underlying sadness in him that I thought a little "Kerri Poppins" could cure.

I found out he was spiritual—a Christian by background, and he was the first guy I had ever even talked about the Lord with. He believed in Jesus as his Savior and had all these stories to share about his spiritual awakenings. I was so intrigued by his stories that I wanted to share some of my own. I wasn't really into talking about God, but by this point I knew it would be nice and proper to date a Christian guy and have someone to sit with at church. I was sick of going alone and leaving alone on Sunday mornings at Mass.

So we talked and talked and talked and kissed and kissed and kissed, and that was that. I had a new boyfriend and the emotional roller coaster left the gates right on schedule. We started dating in that totally gushy, codependent, movie romance way. There was drama on all sides and I loved every minute of it. I was his "angel sent down to save him," we joked, and subconsciously I was buying into that very idea.

I tried to be the domestic goddess I had portrayed myself as. One night I told him I'd make dinner. What ended up happening was my neighbor Tim prepared the appetizers and I bought a seafood mix in a bag that I poured over rice. I threw the bag away and placed the seafood mix over the rice in a big pot, like I had slaved over it all day. He never knew the difference because my kitchen had that wonderful aroma of home cooking. And I can't believe I didn't burn the rice!

It took a whopping two weeks for us to declare our undying love for each other. (Note to self: Never date anyone more than two weeks unless declaration of undying love has been made.) Neither of us had much money so we'd take long walks on the beach and talk about our hopes and dreams, sparing no detail. I was still working under the "give your heart and 100 percent to every relationship" and that way you can say you tried your best. That's what I learned from the movies, and it always seemed to work for Julia and Meg!

So we connected, and I learned he had dreams of show business and moved out to California to pursue them. We would go look at million dollar houses and talk of the future. We were visionaries with big dreams and not a lot else to back them up. We didn't have God's blessing, and I jumped in so fast my friends were just basically along for the ride. They liked him, but more than a few people commented on how opposite our personalities were. What they wanted to say was, "You guys don't belong together, but we don't know how to tell you!" I came up with the answer, "We balance each other," meaning, "He's a cute guy and he likes me, so leave me alone!" I came up with a lot of answers for myself when I would see things that should have been red flags. I had a man who was trying to change his lifestyle for me and someone I was very attracted to—on the inside and outside—so that was good enough.

People told me he would never change and he'd still be the "party guy," but I was bound and determined to prove them wrong. I found that I had turned into that stereotypical, "I will change him" girlfriend. I thought love—or our emotions—would get us through. It's not like he had asked me to change anything about myself except to be more tolerant of our differences. So we compromised and kept meeting in the middle and then butting heads. We were like oil and water in a lot of ways, but once again, my emotions had taken over any logical side of my brain and there was no turning back. My parents — especially my mother — were happy at the prospect of that long-awaited wedding she had already planned.

As we sailed along in our oblivion, I turned into one of those people I make fun of at the grocery store — the ones who are all over their significant other, cooing and making food choices as a "couple." I was learning about him and he about me, and because we talked about God, I thought I was in a Christian relationship. I suppose technically that was true, but — (a) this was not a guy God picked for me, and (b) I was not behaving myself in a godly manner on any level at all. I just talked about God and how much I loved him and then went on with my own plans.

I went to church alone until one day he decided to join me at Mass. I think I cried because I was so happy. We started attending church together, but honestly, it didn't make any difference in how we were living our lives. We occasionally read a mini devotion. No, let me rephrase that. *I* read a mini devotion and *he* was in the room. In my heart I wanted to have this Christian relationship even though I had no examples in my life of what that was. In fact, I didn't know myself what it looked like.

A friend I went to college with is a feisty, Italian redhead and we had some crazy times on the dance floor. She went off to a big city to be a dancer. Long story short: She fell in love with this totally Christian guy. He didn't lay a hand on her for the longest time. I remember thinking he was gay, to be honest. I didn't know guys like that. They had this totally pure courtship that I watched with intrigue, and eventually they got married. But the whole time I was watching my friend go from the crazy party girl to a godly woman who was submitting her whole life to God's plans. Best of all, she had a partner to help her do it.

I was secretly jealous when I saw how happy she was and what a wonderful relationship they had. She tried to talk to me about making some changes with Jake. She even sent me *Passion and Purity* by Elisabeth Elliot. I thought she was a little nuts and totally condescending. I mean, who was *she* to try to tell me how to live my life? I was the "good one" between the two of us in college, or so I thought. She leads a life of craziness and then at the last minute meets Mr. Church Boy, starts living a new life, and everything turns out perfectly for her. No way! Where is the justice in that?

I read *Passion and Purity* and deep inside I knew it described a real love affair. It was about a relationship based on common values, prayer, and reflection on God's plans for two people. It wasn't like my relationship, which was based on the goose bumps I got when Jake told me I was attractive, or the fact we both loved sushi and country music. I know now God was using my friend to gently plant another seed about his plans for my life. I just didn't like hearing it very much, and old habits die hard. I've never been one to openly admit I was wrong. I started searching the Bible for verses that told me my relationship with Jake wasn't what God wanted. Since there was nothing definitive like, "Kerri, you are wrong," I went on with my rationalizations.

Things with Jake and I were getting rougher after we'd been dating for about a year. I was judgmental about his lifestyle and wanted him to have some sort of "spiritual walk" that I could identify with. Since I was leading such a pristine, godly lifestyle myself, I had all the room in the world to be as legalistic as I wanted. Yeah right.

That summer I was doing the play *Godspell* and Chris, a friend of mine in the show, invited me to her church. It was a little beach church, and she told me they had potlucks and surf days. I was wooed by the food, so I thought I'd drag Jake along and give it a shot.

One Sunday we walked into that church near the beach about ten miles south of LA and my life changed forever. The pastor wore a Hawaiian shirt and pants and when he talked, not only did I stay awake the whole time, I understood exactly what he was trying to convey. He talked for thirty minutes that seemed like only ten. The people there were so cool and real and nobody seemed stuffy or judgmental toward anyone else. So week after week Jake and I would walk into this little beach church and hear the Word of God.

Have you ever walked into a place where the Holy Spirit was so strong you immediately were moved by it? I was hearing a new kind of music that they didn't play in my Catholic church or my mom's Presbyterian church either. It was called praise music, and when I listened to the words of these songs, more often than not, I would find myself crying. (This was the place where they even had boxes of Kleenex in the aisles.)

I didn't really know why, but there was some kind of cleansing going on inside my heart. I would be moved to ask God's forgiveness for things in my life. I was starting to see a picture of the life God had for me … the peace God had for me. I could see it in the people at this tiny church. They came from all walks of life — people who had dealt drugs, worldly Hollywood entertainers, those that had practiced other religions, some who had prison records — you name it. But that was all in the past and they were now new creations. The thing I loved is that nobody was ashamed to talk about their past. They called it their "testimony," and it was always to give glory to God for delivering them from a pit of some sort.

One night I was complaining for about thirty minutes after a show to my friend Chris about all Jake's faults, problems, and sins and why he was ruining our relationship because he wouldn't change. She just told me to go home and take a long hard look at myself and get down on my knees and ask God to reveal what he would change about me. She told me not to talk about Jake anymore and to take care of myself. I was floored to say the least, but Chris was never one to mince words. She called me out on several glaring things in my life that were not exactly godly behavior. Just because in the world's eyes I was this good church girl didn't mean it was really true. Reluctantly I took her advice and asked God to show me what needed to go in my life.

"Look out kiddies, we're in for a bumpy ride!" as my girl Betty Davis once said. I was convicted on a level I had never been before. I started to see my joking and gossip about others as something that wasn't good, even if I thought it was harmless before and it got me lots of laughs. My personality actually started to change. I thought about everything differently. A college girlfriend and I had had a falling out over the phone about something stupid, and we hadn't talked in months. God kept telling me I had to apologize to her. The whole time I was convinced I was right, but God was saying "right" didn't matter. I didn't want to deal with it, but it kept bugging me. I finally wrote her a letter apologizing. It was really, really hard but I felt better after I did it. This is one example of the many changes God was making in my life. A year before I would have *never* sucked it up like that. I would have gone to my grave still angry with my ego intact. But that is totally the opposite of what God wanted from me.

I started to see the error of my ways with Jake, but I knew I didn't have the strength to make these changes in our relationship alone. We were in some huge fight at the time, and we went about three days without talking. When we finally came back together, you know what happened? He said he had been doing some praying and the Lord told him the error of our ways, and we needed to start over and try to have a more God-honoring relationship. He said he wasn't respecting me before, and he wanted to do it right. What? I thought I was dreaming! I didn't believe God could work in both our lives at the same exact time! But then again ... he is God! He parted the Red Sea, didn't he? I was overjoyed to say the least, and Jake and I started over to the best of our abilities. We were nowhere near perfect but our hearts were in the right place, for sure.

I started telling my friends about God in my life and all that was going on. Guess what? Most of them thought I was off my rocker. They started seeing changes in me, and I wasn't too popular anymore. I definitely wasn't as fun at the bars on the Hermosa Pier! Some of them even rejected me and stopped calling. This was a painful process and one I didn't count on. I didn't run to God for comfort. I still went to people like Jake and new friends in my church. Maritza, a wonderful woman in my church, began guiding, mentoring, and caring for me, and gently helped me get my life on the right track for the very first time. It wasn't easy, and it didn't happen overnight. She never gave up on me and neither did my Father God. He was there every step of the way.

Jake and I still had different ideas on how our relationship would look. We struggled and we fought, but I was turning it over to God ... or at least giving it my best shot. We started going to church events and more often than not, I was dragging him there. I made new friends with people who had been right where I was. It was a whole new world for me. It was a tough year for Jake and me, but God definitely had my attention like never before.

27

next!

When I was dating Jake I always said if we broke up it would be over for me. I didn't want to go through all the drama of a new relationship—introducing that person into my life and to my family and friends and vice versa. It takes too much work! With Jake I knew the "dance" and we were very comfortable in our roles as partners even though we were not the best possible match for each other—and deep down I knew it.

Most people at my church thought we were engaged. "How could you be dating that long and not be?" they wondered. We even went to a couples small group where everyone was married. We acted like we were married and had all the fights of a married couple, just not the commitment.

Most Christian couples I knew met when they were twelve and dated for about two seconds. Not us! Well, I see how I was praying for God's will, and he wasn't about to let me walk down the aisle with Jake, no matter how hard I tried. I'd pray for a sign from God and he'd give me one; I'd ignore it and ask again. I just wanted it to work so badly. Sure we fought, but he was a good guy and a Christian ... *and* good looking. He fit the bill. We went to couple's events together; we even went to pre-marital counseling once. My pastor told us to read the *Preparing for Marriage* workbook. So I took it on a picnic to the beach in Malibu, and we got in a fight and Jake threw it in the ocean! Ahh ... don't you just love the moody, emotionally unstable, bad boy types?

We didn't see eye to eye on things, but we were in love and love is blinding. One day when someone challenged me about Jake, asking if he was all I'd ever dreamed of, I almost choked. I froze. I realized at that moment that I couldn't say yes. I knew no one is perfect, but I did want someone perfect for me and I wanted to be the same for him ... but Jake and I weren't perfect for each other—not even close. I'll never forget that day. I started to rationalize all the reasons he was right for me, and I really heard myself for the first time. I sounded so stupid too. "Uh, well ... he's really good looking and he's Christian ... and he goes to church (when I drag him) and he's ... uh ... really good looking."

I was convicted. Did I want God's best for me in a husband or did I want a man I chose? Did I trust God or not? It was time to "walk the walk" not just "talk the talk."

I told Jake my feelings. He was furious because he thought some stranger was putting ideas in my head. He didn't like authority figures! He was basically a rebel without a clue!

Two days later he too was convicted. Wow! God works fast! He broke up with me. I couldn't believe it! I wanted to do it first because my ego is so fragile, but it was actually Jake's idea that we pray and break up and be friends—just to see what God wanted in our lives. Guys are so weird when they pull the "friends" card out of the blue! One minute the sun rises in my smile and you can't wait to spend the rest of your life with me; the next minute you want to be my *friend*? I went along with it because I didn't have a choice.

We called it "taking a break," but I knew it was over. I mourned the relationship and skipped the engagement party of two of our best friends that night. Talk about irony! They had only been dating eight months and God had no problem letting them waltz down the aisle!

ARRRGH! I was so mad and angry at everything that had not gone according to my plans once again! I'm a good actress, but there was no way I was driving to some party alone only to put on that fake "I'm happy for you" face to a bunch of people celebrating love and marriage! Not tonight! I just moped around and ate a lot of sugar!

The next day was weird; it didn't seem real. My life had taken an unplanned detour, and I kept thinking about all of our plans for a life together. Our hopes and dreams were not meant to be. There would be no more Sunday afternoon car rides in rich people's neighborhoods looking at houses we dreamed of having someday. We would never sing songs to the radio and laugh our heads off together again. I knew there was so much I was losing, and it was terribly hard to accept.

My poor mother, who had already planned my *Southern Living* wedding, was going to freak out. Everyone was going to freak out. We had put two years into this relationship and now it was over. I didn't want to face it, but more importantly, I didn't want to be alone. I was supposed to be married by now; I had some catching up to do. I'll just get back on the horse. Perfect! I went straight into autopilot mode. Now who would the lucky bachelor be? Hmmm ... decisions ... decisions.

The night after we broke up I went to a Christian event. Every single man in sight was a possibility because they were all Christians. I had a mission: replace Jake in the next forty-eight hours. This all may have been happening subconsciously, but looking back, I recognize that's what was going on.

I used to have a mad crush on Jeff who was an actor/model friend. He was so good looking that when I was twenty-one my palms would sweat when he sat next to me. Well, he thought of me like a little sister, and we formed a friendship filled with jokes and flirtations. Through the years I got over my crush, but he was still cool and really cute. That night I told Jeff about my breakup. I started thinking of Jeff as dating material again ... only for a second. He had only gotten cuter over the past couple of years for sure.

Another actor friend, Max, was just a kid at twenty-one, but he looked and acted much older. I'd always been secretly attracted to him—me and about a million other girls he knew ... I mean, he loved the Lord and was a sold-out Christian, he was cute, he could sing and play guitar like Dave Matthews—seriously! So I don't know what happened, but I decided that night that young Max would be my next boyfriend. Did he even know what Atari was or listen to 80s music? Had he ever ridden a bike without a helmet or drank water from the tap? No, he was too young for all of that!

Who cared? He was there and he was single. He even walked me out to my car that night and as we were having our usual flirtation, I was certain he liked me. We said our goodbyes, and I went home feeling good about myself again. That was all I needed. I was back in the game!

I was all set. I'd been single twenty-four hours, but everything was going to be okay. I was waiting on God but presenting him with two viable options he could choose from. Mind you, I'd sworn off dating actors, but these were desperate times and all the rules were null and void; and the Christian card trumped the actor card, so it was fine.

My thoughts were racing. I was certifiably mad, obsessed with men and the mission of finding a new boyfriend. Everyone was asking me about my breakup with Jake and I did my best to be chipper and give them the usual spiel—"It's all for the best; we're still friends, etc." I was still questioning the decision in my heart though. How crazy is this? In my search for a perfect 10, I broke up with a good 8 and most people can't even find a 4.

I was given the advice to take some time off from men, just to be alone with God and figure things out. This pastor suggested a six-month hiatus and I bargained him down to three because even that seemed unbearable, but I was game.

I started a three-month hiatus and told everyone that was my plan. This seemed like an eternity, but I was going to stick to it. No dates for three months. This would be a new record. I was in complete denial of how painful it would be to get over Jake. After all, we had spent two years together! Thank God we weren't physically bonded to one another; we had gotten our acts together for the last year of our relationship and this made the breakup so much easier.

I wrote love letters to God in my journal and made a list of what I wanted in a husband:

1. Spiritual leader—Someone who puts God first; who will give our relationship to God's control.
2. Someone who will pray for, and with me, and also read the Bible together; a man open to exploring God's kingdom through fellowship or Bible studies (not just ones I drag him to).
3. A man who will cherish me and make me laugh. This was key because I had to have someone hilarious, and God had to know that already.

After writing all of this in my journal I took a drive and prayed: "God, as long as I'm asking, when you send me someone can I add a few details? Can he be a good dancer, cook, someone who loves to travel, and is also neat?"

So I prayed and waited. I waited on God. But I didn't stop obsessing about every Christian guy I knew. Was he the one? I asked that question about all of them. I weighed the pros and cons in my head and flirted madly with them all.

Now this practice of waiting had not worked so far in my relationships and I knew it, so I wanted to do things God's way. I was so anxious though. I was lonely, sad, and insecure, but I prayed earnestly to God and told him I was trying my best. I submitted my love life to him.

Well, it didn't happen right away. I still tried to maneuver things.

For instance, every time I would see Max, the twenty-one-year-old, I'd practically throw myself in his path and flirt mercilessly, waiting for him to ask me to coffee or something. It never happened—what a shocker!

It seemed Jeff was starting to show some interest in me. He was calling me almost every day and flirting a little more. He even invited me over to his place for dinner. Great, right? No way! I was a wreck. I wasn't ready for real male attention. I was barely out of my relationship with Jake and all those feelings hadn't been dealt with. I freaked out. I'd make plans with Jeff and then cancel. I couldn't handle it. It was dawning on me that I wasn't in a healthy place at all. Looking back, I'm not even sure if Jeff did like me in that way. He might have been trying to be a supportive friend, but I couldn't see things clearly because I was so obsessed with dating.

Finally, God put a stop to it. I knew I was going to see Max and Jeff one night. I got all dressed up, but not enough to look like I tried. We've all been there, right ladies? Jeff was being sweet, as usual, but I was basically ignoring him while waiting for Max. As soon as Max showed up, I walked right over to him and started babbling about nothing. All he asked me was, "How are you?" and I went into this ten-minute monologue of arbitrary details and attempts at humor that made me look like a rambling idiot.

He was quiet at that moment and seemed to have a serious look on his face. I went into my spiel about how great I was doing after the breakup, how healthy I felt, and how I was just great … blah, blah … on and on while he stared at me blankly. Finally, he patted me on the shoulder and said, "That's nice, Kerri. I've gotta go." Okay, *that* was not part of the plan. He was supposed to tell me how great I looked and say, "Hey, maybe we can get coffee later, which will be the start of a meaningful relationship." I had just been dissed by a twenty-one-year-old kid!

I stood there and then Jeff came up from behind me. He immediately looked at me and said, "Kerri, you have a booger hanging from your nose." And he walked away. What? Oh, this is classic. This was an all-time low. Was I on some reality show at the moment? This was so humiliating. God had to be laughing! "Fine," I said. "Fine, God. I'll stop. I'm making a fool of myself anyway, aren't I?" I prayed loudly in my car on the drive home. I'm sure they don't have comedy clubs in heaven; God just gathers the angels around and they watch my love life unfold!

It was at that point that I really submitted it to God—my whole life. Well, at least for a few days.

28

the christian chatroom: tales from the dark side

So picture this: a brisk California evening in December. My boy-friend and so-called love of my life for two years and I had broken up. I was thirty days into my self-imposed three-month dating hiatus. I was so grand about it and announced to anyone who would listen that I was on this "dating cleanse" as if it were the newest diet and was working wonders for my skin.

I went to a Christmas party at the home of my old friend Jason. I met him early on when I came to Los Angeles. The Michigan crowd that I hung with when we all moved out together would be at this party. It was also the same crowd that reminded me of my old Jew-ish love, Steve. Steve and I had this really close group of friends and we would all hang out at Jason's apartment by the beach and have barbecues, watch college football, and just have a great time. I didn't hang out much with them since Steve and I had broken up years ago, but they would be nice to see.

It would also be my first time to meet Steve's fiancée. I had heard so much about her ... not just from him but from everyone, and it was all great stuff. I knew I didn't have feelings for Steve anymore, but it still would be weird. I couldn't picture what this girl would be like.

I put on something sassy and embarked for the party. It's funny how my party attire was a lot less low-cut and form-fitting than it used to be. I was getting conservative in my old age. It was like a little college reunion and everyone was pleasant. We had evolved from beach parties with a keg to actually serving hot appetizers. One of the guys even had on a sweater vest. You better believe it was purchased by his girlfriend.

It seemed the carefree beach crowd was slowly growing up and getting serious. People were engaged and I was ... alone. I was starting over and the prospect of that seemed too much to take. I was different now too. I knew the kind of guy I needed wasn't going to be at a party like this, but nonetheless I'd have a good time. People knew I was much more into my faith these days, but no one really understood it. That was okay. I didn't feel like explaining my new lifestyle choices anyway. I was just there to see some old friends, have some cheese dip, and check out this new woman in Steve's life.

So they walk into the apartment—Steve and Sarah. Steve always knew how to make an entrance, and he still had that smile I remembered. I, of course, put on my best fake LA smile and geared up for the moment of being introduced to his "new love." Did he tell her she was the love of his life and all the other things I once heard? He must have ... they were engaged and she had a huge rock on her finger. Steve was a self-made millionaire, by the way, at a very, very young age. Steve's crowd had now moved on to driving fast cars and talking about trips to the "islands" and buying condos. I was so out of place because I still shopped at the ninety-nine cents store for most of my grocery needs and worked two jobs.

Sarah was cute—not so cute as to be intimidating, but definitely pleasant. She had dark hair and her dress was classic and conservative. She had a warm presence about her; I could tell from just looking at her. I knew this would be awkward, but it had to be done. The three of us stood there and exchanged pleasantries, and then all of a sudden she hugged me and the strangest thing happened. We began talking. It may have started in that fake LA, you're-the-new-fiancée way, but it progressed into a real heartfelt conversation between two women that had cared for the same crazy, mixed-up, goofy man. We talked about his family and how cute his little siblings were and how she had really bonded with his mother. I knew she fit in with his family much better than I ever did. It just seemed to work. Steve had found his soul mate, and I was actually taken aback at how perfect they seemed for each other.

Sarah and I stayed on the couch giggling for quite some time until Steve couldn't take it anymore and came to break it up because he was scared to death about what was being said. They both knew that I had just gotten out of a serious relationship. It was really weird when the two of them gave me some words of encouragement. They were being so sweet and telling me to wait until it was right and I would just know when that person came into my life. I could see they both had done exactly that. It was so obvious how in love they were. I knew she was everything he needed and that she would make him very happy. It was so surreal because I was truly in love with him at one point and now I was happy to see him marrying somebody else. Now where was *my* soul mate?

Well, he certainly wasn't at the party, and I made an early exit after I had all my obligatory conversations and explained to everyone that my recent ex and I had just broken up, but I was fine and it was for the best, blah … blah … blah. I left with a smile on my face that night, and Steve actually hugged me as he walked me out to the car. I felt this sense of total closure from him. I knew we had gone through some amazing, crazy, emotional times together, but we were both going to be all right.

When Steve and I dated, we were so young and naïve. We shared so many experiences; both being in a new state with hopes and dreams. We both had such type-A, driven personalities. We were great at parties together but didn't have compatibility for the long haul. He had found someone with a gentle spirit in Sarah. I could tell she calmed him and supported him and even admired the things in him I found beyond annoying. He once said to me he wanted the fairy tale, and it seemed to me he had gotten it ... just not with me.

I drove home and slowly the smile faded from my face as all these thoughts of the evening started flooding into my head. Steve was engaged, and so were a few others from the group. People were settling down into their BMW-driving, fancy job, sweater vest-wearing, cider-drinking lives, and where was I going? I was a starving actress living paycheck to paycheck, chasing this dream of mine and now I was doing it alone. Alone! This was ridiculous and had to be some cruel joke. I was the one that was supposed to be making eggnog with my hot fiancé, throwing fabulous parties in our beach house and starting our dream-like life together. I wasn't supposed to drive along the ocean remembering all the romantic walks and talks I had there. I remembered plans that were made ... promises to be together "forever" that seemed to just slip away. How come forever never seemed to happen for me?

Every time I had gotten wrapped up in some romantic entanglement, I made sure it was very dramatic so it fit my relationship profile. I just wanted the security that I thought some man could give me by telling me he loved me forever and would never leave, and all the other validations I thought I needed to be emotionally happy. Why couldn't I see that only God could give that to me? Even if I did get married, there's no guarantee the guy would be around forever. People come in and out of this world as God chooses, so why did I think my life would be any different?

I wanted it to be right and didn't want to settle, but now was I settled into a life of attending holiday parties dateless? It had been thirty days and it was too much to take. I was the girl with the boyfriend ... the one with the great story ... whether he was down the street or across the country. I never had a Valentine's Day without roses or a New Year's Eve without a crush or date of some sort. I always had someone in my life and on my heart, and now it was literally just me for the first time since I was five years old and I told

Brandon Duck I loved him on the kindergarten playground. (By the way, he told me he loved me too.)

I talked to God loudly in my car about it. If he talked back, I wasn't in the mood to hear him through my rumblings. Life didn't seem fair. I missed my recent ex, Jake, but I didn't want him back. God had clearly shown me we weren't right for each other. In fact, we had been trying to do the "friends" thing, and the weekend before we were driving home from church together. I was driving and missed an exit. He, in his typical fashion, got really mad at me and lost his cool. Instead of arguing back as I had in the past, I started laughing. I couldn't stop and it was making him madder by the second. He wanted to know why I was laughing so uncontrollably. I knew it was because God was showing me that this guy was not someone for me. I no longer have to deal with his dislike of my driving skills or any of the other things that drove me crazy about him. I was free! I felt like a thousand-pound weight had been lifted off my shoulders and I actually felt joy. I dropped him off at his house and laughed all the way home.

Back to my Saturday night drive home after the party. I came home to my apartment, got something chocolate out of the fridge, and sat down to check my emails as usual to feed my need for validation. Maybe I'd hear from one of my guys (Doug, Justin, whoever) with a quick "Hello and hold your head up" note to lift my spirits. Both of my Jewish loves had moved out of Los Angeles by then, so there was no running to Justin's for his famous barbeque and no late-night coffee shops in Santa Monica with Doug—comparing each other's finer qualities. It was about 1:30 in the morning, and I really don't know where the idea came from but I decided to look up the words "Christian dating" online. And then it appeared: Christian Café.

Dear Kerri,

Are you sick of driving home alone from holiday parties where you see your former boyfriend who is now happily in love, leaving you no choice but to be sitting by a computer at 1:30 a.m.? Are you

*tired of great guys that will dance with you on a Saturday night
but not want to be anywhere near church on a Sunday morning?
Are you sick of being the spiritual leader in a relationship? Are you
wondering where your hot Christian soul mate is—the one who
will make you eternally happy and solve all your problems? Well,
you've come to the right place. With a click of the mouse you can
design your perfect mate, right down to his height, weight, and hair
color. We will find him and deliver him right to your computer photo
profile, and all in a matter of seconds. He will have no flaws and
will worship the ground you walk on, in that godly-appropriate-
Christian way. It's that simple. Just fill out a sample profile and try
it for ten days absolutely free. What do you have to lose? You're here,
aren't you?*

Sincerely,
ChristianCafe.com

Well, it may not have been worded exactly that way but that is
how I read it. And being the type-A personality that I am, I decided
that now would be the perfect time to fill out the personality profile.
I wouldn't have to include any personal information or a photo. I had
heard about people meeting online, but to be honest, these were not
the kind of guys I would have considered to be my type. I mean, if
my ego wasn't in such a state of disarray and if it wasn't almost 2:00
a.m., I wouldn't have done it, but I was clinically desperate and had
waited on God long enough. I mean thirty days ... come on! And I
decided that if I made it to February before I actually met someone
in person, I would have completed my three-month hiatus. It was all
falling into place and I was off to the races.

This was better than the movie *Weird Science* and it was actually fun. I told the computer exactly the kind of flawless man I was
looking for—geographically desirable and devilishly handsome. I
filled out my personality profile using my usual comedic flare, with
a touch of that sweet vulnerability that would make me seem acces-

sible. After all, I wasn't including a picture, so my answers had to be good. I think I was a little too honest, though. They asked where I thought a good first date would be and I wrote, "The police station to get fingerprinted."

Here are some quotes from my actual profile:

Describe the type of relationship you are looking for.

First of all, I'm looking for someone who is willing to lie about how we met! Ha! Okay, I'm not supposed to lie; lighten up, it's a joke. I want someone who is totally sold out for God and wants to be a part of my crazy journey called life. I want a guy who is hilariously funny, witty, a hopeless romantic, and someone who is not afraid to be absolutely crazy. I want a spiritual leader who will pray with me and for me, and someone who sees the best in people.

Describe your Christian faith.

I can't believe I'm even writing on this website, but here goes. I want to conquer the world for God. He rocks! And I want to reach people and share what God has done for me. I'm growing and learning more each day. I'm looking for someone to be with, to mature with in my walk with the Lord, and to have fun with at the same time. God knows my heart. Right now he is teaching me patience — which is why I should not be signing on here; I am supposed to be "waiting on him to find me someone." God laughs at me all the time when I try to take matters into my own hands. He always knows best and never lets me down.

(So it's like I was on there to meet someone but still not comfortable with the idea. I had to have my disclaimer that I didn't think this was God's way for me to meet someone, but I was trying it anyway.)

Describe your current occupation.

I own my own business. I don't want to say too much; if my friends are on here they will recognize me. I am blessed with my job because it allows me to pursue my other passions. I could see myself in ministry someday if that is what God wants for me, but I could also see myself as a really good housewife.

(This was written three years ago—before I ever thought of this book or the stand-up comedy ministry that I'm in today. Funny how God works.)

What are some of your personal goals in life?

Personal goals in life would be to find an amazing husband, have a family, and spend our lives dancing in the kitchen and serving God. I want a family that God will be proud of. I would like to use my performing gifts in order to reach people and tell them about God's love. I also want a house by the beach with a hammock. I've always wanted a hammock.

What caused your last relationship to end? What have you learned?

Wow! They don't mess around with these questions, do they? Well, I guess it was just a feeling that this person was not God's best for me. I want God's choice for me and not mine. I need someone a little crazier and more romantic. I'm willing to wait. I want it the traditional way—no games.

I don't want to date just to date. Being intentional is important to me. (That meant a kiss equals a marriage proposal.) It's like my pastor says, "Be the right person and stop looking for the right person." Or, as my dad told me, "Hon, stop looking for 'Mr. Right.' One day you will probably trip over him in an elevator!"

(Okay, I have to interject here for a moment ... is the irony of my profile killing you? The traditional way ... no games ... I'm willing to wait. I crack myself up because I'm doing the exact opposite of all that by pouring my heart out at 3:00 a.m. to some computer! God had to be having a good laugh that night! Or was he sad for me?)

So now I was officially proactively seeking my mate in that "puttin' it out there at 3:00 a.m. on the internet" kind of way. I had opened Pandora's box and all chaos was about to break loose.

So there it was—the blueprint of the perfect man just staring at me in black and white. I was exhausted, so I went to bed.

29

he will reward you with riches

The next morning I woke up and immediately ran to my computer to "play" on this new website and see if my husband was waiting inside my computer screen for me. It was like Christmas morning with all the emails and pictures of men, large and small, from all over the world. My inbox was flooded with everything from cheesy lines I've heard in bars, to marriage proposals and well-crafted sincere letters telling me why God told them I was to write them back.

The next few days were a thrill ride of validation. I received emails from all around the world—from men that were persuaded I was meant to be their wife. I wrote back to all of them at first. Then I decided to reply only to the ones with cute pictures and good profiles—it was a flurry of emails that took up an extreme amount of time that could have been spent more productively. But I had that addictive personality and this was right up my alley.

People would just lay their hearts out on these sites, I think, because the risk is so minimal, and so are the chances you'll ever really meet someone in person. I took the superficial route. If I didn't like a picture, I would not respond. I was on a mission and not about to waste anyone's time. I think I originally sent "No thank yous" to everyone, but soon that became tiring. I decided to just focus in on my potential loves — the cute ones — only.

It was a bit obsessive compulsive at the same time, giving all my attention to a little computer screen for hours a day. I was emailing people from all over the country, and my validation needs were being met all at once. I was having a ball but not really moving closer to my goal of that perfect man and the house on the beach with a hammock. After a few emails with one person — when it came time to meet — something just "told" me it wasn't right. Maybe "that something" was when the person brought up that he was in prison. (Not that I'm not open to that, but if he's in for ten to twenty years, I don't have the time.) The guys would start out normal and charming and get weird or boring. And no one could keep up with my witty email repartee. I thought I was particularly charming online!

One day I was playing around and reading profiles, and I came across this one guy who liked 80s music, had never been married, loved to cook, liked to take walks on the beach (everyone writes that no matter how close to the beach they live; it's required), and had some other cool qualities that caught my eye. Mostly, I loved the wit and humor in his profile. One of the questions on the profile was, "What are your goals?" He answered with, "Eat junk food and watch TV." Another question was, "Why did your last relationship end?" He replied, "It's complicated. She was a circus midget and I'm six feet tall." I loved it!

Of course, I emailed him and we started chatting online. That's when I realized Mr. Perfect lived in Canada! Nobody lives in Canada! That's where everyone's imaginary girlfriend or boyfriend lives. When someone would come back to school in eighth grade with a steamy summer romance, the person always happened to be modeling somewhere far off in Canada. This was ridiculous! He was thousands and thousands of miles away. But do you think that was going to stop me and fate? No way!

We emailed back and forth for about two hours. He was hilarious and I was in rare form myself. We tried to play this internet thing off as something we weren't really into and just checked out on a dare. We emailed and emailed and emailed. I think I skipped meals that next week just waiting for the next sentence from my "man in the box." We had scary things in common like ... we both ate food ... wore clothes ... listened to music. It was uncanny. This was love; we were sure of it. I think in reality we were just two normal people on that site who were happy to find someone we could actually communicate with on a higher level.

I told my mentor, Maritza, about him and the site. She was encouraging me to slow down and seek the Lord, so I prayed. I asked God for guidance, and then I would go sign on that darn computer again and there he would be. His name was Rich and he worked in the marketing world. I was really into this guy and it worked out well that he was far away, because to the outside world, I was still officially on my "dating fast." I was convinced this internet thing did not count so I was fine. Our emails turned into phone calls, and I found myself in an intense long-distance relationship. How did that happen when I'd never even met this guy? I can't even imagine the looks on my friends' faces when I started telling them about my "Canadian love."

I remember being in Las Vegas with my sorority sisters and announcing that I broke up with my last boyfriend of two years and had found a brand new boyfriend online in a matter of thirty days, and he was from Canada! They were all calm and cool. But how humiliating this was for me deep down now that I think about it! I had become that girl ... you know the one who can't get a date in her own country and has to make up some imaginary boyfriend from Canada. Come on! But I was smitten nonetheless and so was he.

He would send me little gifts from Canada—pictures of him and his family. I even told my parents about him. We talked all the time on the phone and I felt like I knew him. Also, I thought this was the perfect way for me to behave myself physically because there was no possible way to screw up. This *had* to be from God.

We talked about our relationship with God, traded Bible verses, and I felt really "holy" about the whole thing. This relationship was in true "Kerri fashion." I was so caught up in the fantasy of this guy. The true reality that he lived in Canada never really sunk in. He talked of moving to California someday. I was expecting him to propose and offer to buy me an island next, like Todd had offered. After a month or two of this madness and no plans for a visit from either of us, I began to feel like God might not be as involved in this relationship as I had thought.

One Sunday, in the midst of all of this, I went to my church and received prayer from some wonderful ladies. As one lady was praying about my life and my future she said, "God will reward you with riches." I said, "What? Can you please repeat that?" She did. I heard it loud and clear—she said, *"Riches!"* Well, hot dog! I had my sign! I knew God wanted me to be with Rich, my Canadian romance, all along and now it was confirmed—in a church, no less. I floated home and turned on my computer to email Rich. Funny how we can interpret prayer and signs from God just about any way we choose, huh?

Well, things were moving along with Rich, but he wasn't making any moves to visit me and the "phone thing" was getting old. Sign—or no sign—I went back on the internet to view some other options—more local. I had still been emailing on that site the whole time I was getting to know Rich, but not with the same vigor as before. Now I was back with a vengeance.

30

the real dark side begins

After the realization of how far away Canada was, I was back on the website looking for someone who lived in America. I got a couple emails from an older guy in Nashville. He was pleasant looking and seemed to really have his act together. We'll call him Monte. I had to admire his persistence. He told me he was always in LA on business, and he'd like to take me to dinner. The thought of an actual date seemed so nice that I was open to it. It had been almost three months, so I was allowed, and he always talked of the finest places to dine. I think I was more excited about the food than about Monte. I never really said yes or no. We just exchanged a few emails.

Monte was really involved in his church and had many stories about his faith and his family. He talked of his fishing trips with his dad and church outings with friends. He was very well off financially, or so it seemed, from owning his own business. My gut kept telling me this guy wasn't right, but for whatever reason, he would always email me and I'd respond. Even so, every time he'd ask me out I'd give some reason I was busy that weekend. Something was definitely holding me back from meeting this guy. I remember having coffee one night with my friend Trista and actually telling her about Monte because I thought maybe he'd be more her type—if he turned out to not be my type.

Another key detail about getting to know Monte is that we had exchanged our real last names. I think I had been talking about my acting and he had gone to some website where my pictures and video were online. What could be the harm in that? Everyone else in America could Google my name and find information on me, right? No big deal. And my trial membership was almost up on the dating site, so I had given a few of the guys my regular email address so we could stay in touch.

I had forgotten I gave my regular email address to Monte, but periodically he would write me and ask why I wasn't responding. I just thought he was a little too needy, so I cut him off completely. He never seemed mad, but I thought he'd get the hint by then and stop writing. He'd write at weird times like on a Friday night and say things like, "I bet a nice girl like you is home tonight, huh?" and a variety of other attempts at humor. He'd always end the emails with another invitation to see me. These emails went on for about a month on my regular account, and if I ever signed on to that Christian dating website, he would immediately write me on there as well. I was slowly getting sick of that internet site anyway. Prince Charming had not appeared, and there weren't any possible candidates surfacing at the time.

One Monday morning I was working from home and my office phone rang. I picked up the receiver and heard a man's low voice on the other end who was asking for Kerri. I said, "This is she." He then proceeded to launch into some of the crudest, raunchiest language I had ever heard. I immediately hung up and thought it was some sick joke one of my so-called friends was playing on me. The phone rang again and angrily I asked, "Who is this?" He said he was "the guy from the bar" this past weekend. Coincidentally, I was out with my friends at a birthday party at a bar but hadn't given my number out, much less talked to anyone new. He then proceeded to threaten me and tell me he was coming over to my house to hurt me in a violent, crude way.

I was in shock! And then all of a sudden an email popped up on my computer from some Hotmail address that I had never seen before. It was from the same sick guy, making more threats in a sexual manner. Immediately, I wrote him back and said, "You don't know who you're dealing with! My Italian uncle is a cop and I am going to call him right this instant!" Okay, so I didn't have an uncle who was a cop, but I did have some Italian uncles and I had used that one before to scare guys so I hoped that would do the trick. I was in panic-shock mode and didn't know what else to do. This guy emailed me back with more disgusting language and didn't seem threatened at all. He seemed to be amused at my disgust.

My phone rang again and I knew it was him. I didn't answer, but I sent an email to him telling him not to call my "office" ever again. He replied, "Who are you kidding? I know you work from home."

I think I fell off my chair in sheer terror. Was this guy across the street watching me? Was this someone I knew? I called my building manager, Harold, and he came over. I was calm at this point, yet totally numb. This was like something out of a Lifetime television movie! What had I done to deserve this kind of treatment, and when would Meredith Baxter Bernie show up as my long lost mother? Okay, back to the story.

The phone rang again and Harold answered it. The guy asked for me and when Harold said I was not home, he laughed and hung up. We called the police to file a report. That day was such a blur. I drove to my church because I had a drama group rehearsal. I was so shaken I could barely talk. I told my friends what was happening and they were concerned. When we checked my email from the church office, there were more threats from him, saying that he was coming over to my place and that if I called the cops he would kill me. I won't go into all the details of the emails, but they were sick and wrong and horrible on a whole new level.

Whoever was writing them was severely disturbed. When I finally talked to a detective, he told me not to answer any of the emails and also not to answer my phone for that day. They got all the information and said they would put a trace on his email address and get back to me with details.

All that day I couldn't walk, talk, or breathe. As I drove my car I was looking over my shoulder at every driver on the road wondering if this madman was in the vicinity. I had some friends come over to my apartment that day and stay with me. I was planning a trip home to Georgia that week, so I felt like I would be safer there. My mind kept spinning, wondering who would do this to me. Who would be so angry at me to want to act in this manner? My whole life had changed in an instant.

The detectives called me that afternoon and said they had traced the Hotmail address to a computer in Nashville and wanted to know who I knew in that city. I knew it had to be Monte, that guy I met on the internet who wouldn't leave me alone. I gave them all the details about him and the Christian chatroom and everything I could think to tell them. I realized my home office number was listed, and he must have just called and asked for my name. It was that easy.

I got a couple more emails from him, which I didn't respond to, and there were some more hang-up calls on my office machine over the next week. I had a male office assistant answering my phone for the next week and no more verbal threats were made.

The police were waiting to hear from me about whether I wanted to press charges or not. The detective scared the living daylights out of me with his stalker stories. He said I could get a restraining order—that was about it at this point since he had never physically harmed me. Well, not yet anyway. I didn't know how to handle it. The detective told me guys like this want attention and if you don't give it to them, sometimes they just move on. I didn't want him moving on to someone else, but I didn't want to get him angrier at me and cause him to come out to LA like he said he would.

It was just an awful situation and I needed God more than I ever had. I had nothing else—no one else. My family couldn't protect me, my friends could only offer their sincere concern, and even the authorities couldn't control this guy from coming to LA one day and looking me up. All I could do was fall on my knees and cry out to God. "Help me, God! Please help me! Deliver me from this evil!"

I kept reciting the Psalms and any verse I could think of about the Lord being "my Protector" and "my Refuge." I kept going back to Psalm 91:9–10, "If you make the Most High your dwelling—even the Lord, who is my refuge—then no harm will befall you, no disaster will come near your tent." I clung to those words with everything I had. I had to find my rest and peace in him. If I was to get on with my life, I didn't have a choice.

It was a battle every minute of every day not to give in to the fear that was plaguing me. It's an indescribable feeling to someone who hasn't experienced their very life being threatened. All the things in the world that seemed important fell completely by the wayside. I just wanted to have peace again in order to live one day without fear. I had a lot of people praying for me.

I went home to Georgia and told my parents everything that was going on. My mother freaked out and my father had his own ideas on how to handle the guy. I actually feared for this man's life if my dad ever found out who he was. Of course, my dad immediately utilized his contacts from his business days and got on the phone with the head of the Nashville police department and the FBI in Tennessee. They found out information about the guy and the police called him and told him they were on to his activities. The guy they called denied everything, saying that it must have been one of his employees on his company computer. I knew it was him and that he was lying.

When I got back to California, the calls and emails stopped. I decided not to press any charges and just prayed that this whole thing was finally over. It was, but I would never be the same.

It's "funny" how important God and his Word become when

everyone else fails you or cannot help you. He gave me peace like I had never experienced. Looking back, in a way I long for that time when it was literally just God and me getting me through my day. I had nothing but him to hold on to and he was there every step of the way. It pains me to think how I slowly let that closeness to God slip away as my life went back to "normal." It took a tragedy in life to make me realize what was really important—I hope I made some changes that stuck.

About a month later I was in church and the pastor asked people to share any stories about what God was doing in their lives. I stood up in front of the congregation and told the story of how God delivered me from that horrible nightmare and how clinging to him made me stronger than I had ever been. I knew then that if I had God, there was nothing we couldn't handle together. That was the first time I spoke in front of a Christian audience intimately about my life. It felt good and I had no idea that God was preparing me for many more speeches to come.

31

current events

Okay! Okay! I'm waiting, I'm waiting! I'm going on eight months now. During this time I've started journaling more to God instead of to myself. I write down my feelings and dreams and put them out there for him to deal with. So I feel like I have to talk about Rob—a situation that I thought could be an end to my "hiatus"! He was the "it" guy in college—at least in my music program. All the girls loved Rob because he was tall, dark, and sang like Harry Connick Jr. Seriously, when we would hear him at his recitals singing "One for My Baby (And One More for the Road)" wearing the fedora hat and trench coat, it was all over. I remember my friend Greta and I coming back to the sorority house swooning like schoolgirls for hours! He was a bona fide celebrity in my mind.

I could never talk to him without stuttering except with the help of some Boone's Farm wine one night. I was at a musical theater party with this one guy I was dating and he was being a real jerk. I haven't included him in this book because that whole relationship was based on the fact that my college friend Tiffini said, "Every girl in Grand Plains loved Mason Biley," and no one could tie him down. So off I went to conquer, and I regret dating him to this day. He was a straight guy who got into musical theater mainly to pick up girls!

And to top it off, he thought he was James Taylor and would proceed to serenade me with these awful renditions of love ballads. It was horrible! "Fire and Rain" is now completely ruined for me! Not to mention I found he was cheating on me with one of my so-called musical theater friends.

Well, being Italian I've always fought that streak of vengefulness that gets me into trouble. When I found out he was cheating on me, it also happened that this other girl was playing Chava in the production of *Fiddler on the Roof* that I was involved with. I was the choreographer, and she buddied up to me to cast her in this role so she could have this big dance solo in the second act! It's traditionally called the "Chava Ballet," and it's where she leaves her Jewish family to marry a non-Jew, and the family joins in the last minute of the dance for a dramatic climax. Well, I waltzed into rehearsal one day and said, "I have news. Now the 'Chava Ballet' is going to be a full group number with all of the family members in it from the beginning, and it's also going to be done in shadows behind a black screen for effect! No one will be seen except in the shadows! I think it will be just brilliant!" The look on her face was priceless! Okay, I know that wasn't Christian behavior and I hope I've moved on, but let me just state for the record, that was years and years ago! Enough said!

So back to the party, and I'm with Mason and he's checking out every other girl in sight. I was twenty-one and decided that this Boone's Farm pink wine might help me enjoy my evening. It seemed to be doing the trick for everyone else. Besides, these musical theater parties could get a little crazy with all the people belting out show tunes! Then from the corner of my diluted eye I see Rob sitting quietly in a chair in the middle of the party. I decided to march up to him, sit right on his lap—uninvited—and proceed to tell him how attractive all the girls thought he was, sparing no details until he looked at me and said, "Well, thank you, Kerri," which was accompanied by this blank stare as if to say, "Could you please remove yourself from my lap, you foolish girl!" My current boyfriend said,

"Uhhh ... Kerri, are you done yet? Are you ready to go?" And off we went. Needless to say, that current relationship ended shortly thereafter. I think that was the last conversation I had with Rob and the last Boone's Farm I ever drank. (FYI—pink stuff should not be consumed in large quantities and drinking is highly overrated. I'd rather be the "good girl" who actually remembers her stories.)

Fast forward five years. Rob is in New York and I heard through the grapevine he's a Christian. That's all—no details. Well, what do you think I did? I got on that computer faster than greased lightning and sent him an email saying, "Hi. Um, it's Kerri from college. I don't know if you remember me, but I heard you love Jesus and so do I ... ⁹ blah, blah ... let's get married," or something like that. Okay, so I didn't mention marriage—exactly—but it was subliminal because as we know, subtlety has always been my strong suit. Ha!

So anyway, a week later he sent me a very sweet, cordial email telling me how he gave his life to God a couple years back and is so happy now. Truly, it was great news, and I wrote him back a few times. Every time he'd write me, I'd write him that same day. Although he didn't ask, I even sent him pictures of me and friends in Los Angeles, just to ensure he would fall madly in love with me. I mean, obviously that's where this was going, right? I've been single all these years and obviously God is going to give me the hottest guy there was in college. I'm so glad we're on the same page!

One small detail ... I don't really know Rob that well, and he doesn't know me at all. We never talked much in school, and after a couple emails I'm planning our relationship. It's a disease, I tell you! My friends and I call it "decorating." Whenever we start dating a new guy and things are going smoothly, we start decorating our imaginary homes in our heads. Once my friend Tracy even went as far as buying her new boyfriend sheets for his bed—assuming of course that she would be using them someday. When they broke up, she obsessed about him by looking into his window with binoculars like in a bad *Laverne and Shirley* episode. Guess who was there to help? Yep, me. That's what friends are for … to encourage each other's neuroses!

But isn't it true how we women are such planners? We can visualize an entire relationship with all of its ups and downs before it even begins. I'm better than I used to be; with some conscious effort, I can stop the insanity before it gets out of hand in my pretty little head.

Anyway, Rob and I actually struck up an email friendship, and it was nice getting to know him. All I knew before was that he was handsome and would probably serenade me nightly as we put our 2.5 children to bed in our newly remodeled beach home. Like that wasn't enough. For all I knew he was engaged, but I hadn't asked and was not too concerned, because if he was the one for me, God would stir his heart.

The reason I bring up this silly story is that I'm realizing my impatience hasn't gone away, but with the Lord's help, I've learned to control my words, emotions, and actions better and I get into trouble less often. I don't think it will ever be easy or that God will turn me into the shy, demure, southern belle my mother wanted so badly. But it's good because I have more peace and confidence, not just in myself but in the Lord and what he's putting together in my life. I know it's going to turn out great! We'll see, won't we?

32

dog lover

I hit an all-time low tonight and I didn't even realize it! I thought I was doing so well too! I need to preface this story by telling the truth—I don't like dogs. Not big dogs, not little dogs. Not cats either. My friend asked me the other day what I thought of cats and the first thing out of my mouth was, "I think they are a waste of air." "Honest?" "Yes!" Will this win me many friends? No, I just don't have an affection for anything furry except my life-size Winnie the Pooh.

So I was walking at the beach with my friend Trista and she waves to this hot-looking guy. She says, "There's my friend, the one I wanted to set you up with." He was my type—dark eyes, great smile, nice build. And with him are these two *large* dogs. I can't believe the words that came out of my mouth as I actually risked my life to reach down and pet one of the furry creatures. "Hi, baby!" *Hi, baby?* Can you believe I was trying to fake being a dog lover? How insane and completely transparent; even the dog looked at me as if to say, "Who do you think you're fooling?" I stood there making small talk, risking my life for fear I would get my hand bitten off, only to find out they weren't even his dogs. I was being a total idiot trying to use "dog language!" He was playing Frisbee with them and their owner was a cute blonde beach chick whom I didn't even notice until it was too late. She was that "dog-loving, eat-a-fat-free-brownie, work-out type of girl." I knew I could never compete with her! It was a total disaster! When will I learn? When will I *ever* learn?

33

why i don't go to trendy bars

I was doing okay—not great, but okay—for being officially single for eight and a half whole months. It was an all-time record! That is until my good friend Tara flew into town from New York for the weekend.

Tara is a wonderful girl and we've been through a lot together. Many of the "old days with Tara and the girls" revolved around going out in large groups to trendy bars. It was quite the ritual indeed. After carefully applying our makeup, putting on our favorite outfit, and playing with our hair to make it just perfect, we would head out to the local beach bars. It was just like the frat parties in college, except these guys had apartments instead of dorm rooms, and they had jobs to brag about instead of how much they could bench press.

We would go to these places where the guy/girl ratio was five to one, and we would flirt shamelessly with whomever we met and spend hours of enjoyment dancing and trying to get the attention of the "Mr. Right Now" of that evening. Afterward, we'd head out around two in the morning, stop for doughnuts or pizza, and have plenty of stories to relive the next morning. It was the best of times; it was the worst of times. Oh, to be so carefree again.

Looking back I realize those times weren't as "carefree" as I like to remember. It was annoying to be the only one wanting to leave at midnight to go home but being afraid my girlfriends would make fun of me because I was being a "grandma." I still was known as a "good girl" comparatively, but really I was all about fitting in so I begrudgingly made it to a respectable 2:00 a.m. and came home with everyone else.

Well, obviously a lot has changed for me since that time, and my old friends see it in my lifestyle choices, but I don't think they understand it. I still try to fit in, but I've outgrown so much of what used to be fun for me. I've changed the way I spend my time, and I hang out with new people who don't think we need to be out at bars all night to have a good time. I've lost a lot of old friends who now deem me as "boring." It really hurts, so I tell myself "I'm so mature." Not really. I learned tonight that I could fall right back into that lifestyle without missing a beat. And just what was it that proved my theory? A guy, of course! My weakness, my hormones, a great smile on a dark-haired charmer ... and it's over for me.

We ran into some frat boys we knew in college. They were very cute and successful and lawyers and internet gurus and so forth. And I saw Blake. The only way to describe him is funny, cocky, good looking, and able to keep up with my verbal sparring and cracking of jokes every second that I like to do when I'm nervous. In college he was known as the good dancer. Back then we shared a few "magical" moments on the dance floor to the likes of Michael Jackson's "PYT" or maybe some Marvin Gaye. Who knows? It was too long ago but I didn't forget him. Everyone loved Blake and that made him all the more attractive to me. Alas another challenge ... how I loved a challenge.

He was trouble with a capital *T*, and he still had "that something" I found irresistible. We exchanged quips and stories and it was fun ... really fun until my friend Tiffani noticed that dumb look on my face I get when I'm in awe of someone. I was right back to the frat parties, trying to be witty and then suddenly aware of the pimples on my face, that my hair was in braids, and that maybe my oversized orange sweater and striped pants weren't too sexy. He was kinda with a girl and I was jealous; I wanted all of his attention. He probably was not walking with the Lord, yet I wanted to ask him to ask me out so I could convert him, get married, and live happily ever after. I thought I was over that part of my life ... but I guess not. One night in a crowded bar filled with lonely people putting on happy faces and checking each other out, and I'm right back there with 'em! Embracing it! It was the same old scene ... everyone pretending to be busy but secretly checking everyone else out ... a total meat market and here I was! Blake gave me his card and walked away to play pool with "Trixie" or whatever her name was. I was over it!

I left the bar and was so mad he didn't totally disregard the chick he was with and follow me out to my car. Okay, I get it! God was protecting me from getting into trouble, but my emotions were raging and trouble looks like so much fun. Once again I felt all alone. I started thinking about my outward appearance: Maybe if my hair had been different he would have liked me. My outfits had changed dramatically over the years from what "going out attire" used to be. I had a lot more cleavage back then ... even if it was thanks to one of my famous "water bras"! I looked like Pollyanna tonight. There were all these superficial thoughts running through my head. I know I'm not an eighth grader, but it goes to show you it doesn't take much to make us fall into our old habits. I just cried out to God in my car and told him I needed some help. Loudly!

I got my help and the next morning realized my little episode the night before was pretty harmless and only a momentary loss of my sanity. I don't need to go to places like that if it's going to drive me insane. I have to face facts: I'm just not "trendy" no matter how hard I try. I'm not that girl anymore, and I'm really better off ... or at least in the long run I will be. Right, God? Right? I think I'm right. I'll let you know!

In case you're wondering, I threw Blake's card away. Better safe than sorry.

34

do nice guys really finish last?

I've been out of the dating game for almost nine months. I think God moved me to the bullpen to warm up just to see if I could handle it. I'm doing okay. And then I met a guy—two guys—real Christian guys. Not the kind I just flirt with mercilessly and then send away because they don't believe in God.

Bachelor number one is sweet and handsome, kind, well-spoken, and totally loves the Lord. We'll call him "Sweet John." What else can I say? He's mature and kind of funny and seems to have an interest in me. When I think about him, I smile. He's a bit older and wears "man shoes"—you know—those sandals older guys wear? I'm not into them, but my friends just call me superficial.

Bachelor number two is the dog guy I met on the beach awhile back. Remember when I made a total fool of myself in front of my friend's friend? Yep, it's the same guy. I couldn't get him out of my mind. He's the type of guy I go for. Dark, funny, Christian, charming, and hot! Seriously, the cutest smile, and did I mention that he's hot? He's hot in that dark-Latin, big-muscles kinda way. Okay, so I've heard he's quite the flirt, which I witnessed first-hand last week when we all went out together. We'll refer to this bachelor as "Hot Joe."

So anyway, Hot Joe was really funny and upbeat and we had a great time talking. Several times he casually mentioned getting together with me, but never anything specific. "Hey! When you're down at the beach, if you need some company . . ." Now the old Kerri would have pulled out a napkin and written down my exact schedule and handed it to him. I resisted (good job, Kerri!). I also resisted saying, "This is the part where you ask for my phone number, dummy!"

We parted ways and I came home with that silly perma-grin on my face, which my roommate pointed out as soon as I came in the door. See, Sweet John does not do that for me, even though several people have told me how great he is and that I should be open to him. But I've felt that instant chemistry with every boyfriend I've ever had. Why shouldn't two people have that? I wished I liked Sweet John because he'd already asked me out twice! What's wrong with me? Why is it the ones we want don't want us, and the ones we don't want, do? Murphy's Law? Objectively, Sweet John has all the qualities I look for in a man. He has everything except that extra something I can't put my finger on.

All week I've been thinking about Hot Joe, wondering if he'll step up to the plate, get my number, and call me. I hate waiting! I constantly hope we'll run into each other, but it hasn't happened. And I know my job is to do nothing but sit back and be pursued. This is a godly concept dating back to Song of Songs. Believe me, the world would tell me to take the bull by the horns and put myself out there and let him know I'm interested. First of all, that's not what God wants me to do. Second, I couldn't deal with the rejection. So I'll just hang tight and live my life and see what happens, if anything. I don't really have a choice — I promised God and myself I'd try this thing *his* way. So here goes!

So I saw Hot Joe last night and as usual he was over-flirtatious, complimenting my eyes and everything. I had tried on three outfits, making sure I didn't look overdressed or underdressed or like I tried too hard. Women want that "Oh, I just threw this on and I happen to look fabulous" look. If men only knew what we women go through for them. And as usual, he did not ask me out. I'm annoyed more than intrigued at this point. I don't think anything will happen with him or it would have already. I can tell he just wants to "play around" and that might be fine for his other conquests—but not with me.

This is making me reconsider my stance on nice guys and where they finish. Do they have to finish last? Is there a nice guy out there who can hold my interest and be compatible with me in all the right areas? I have a lot of thinking to do on this one. Nice … what's wrong with nice? Why is it we women want to use adjectives like "hot" and "charming" and "great dresser," but we never want to describe our perfect mate as "nice"… and yet we have to live with this person for the rest of our lives? How far can a great pair of khakis and a J. Crew turtleneck go when he's acting like a jerk? When I think about my friends' husbands whom I admire and even my own father, "nice" would definitely come to mind. Maybe it's something we think the cocky, good-looking single men will morph into when they get married. After they say "I do," they become nice! I doubt it!

35

take me out of the ball game!

Okay, I'm out. I don't want to be in the game anymore. I'd rather be back on the bench; it's nicer and calmer there. I've only been mildly exploring getting back in the dating pool and already I'm going crazy. I went to this party today and saw Hot Joe, the dog guy. As expected, he looked stunning and was unbelievably charming and flirty. He told me I looked pretty and had beautiful eyes. He was shameless.

He kept flirting and flirting, but I was so far to the being-elusive side, I'm sure I came off as a rigid freak. He kept putting his arm around me and I'd jump up and say, "Why are you touching me?" He was being friendly and I kept reading something into his every move. He was totally invading my personal space, and I don't know if other girls are into that, but I was kind of annoyed, especially since he was doing the same to every girl he met. Remember, this guy is a Christian as well. Boundaries, boys. Boundaries. He obviously thinks that's a sports term.

I had to leave, and once again he did *not* ask for my phone number! I was fighting every urge in my being to say, "So when are you going to ask me out, Rico Suave?" There are so many nice guys that are simple and sweet and would not put me through this "cat-and-mouse" game, but am I attracted to them? No, that would be too easy and emotionally sane!

What have I learned taking this nine-month hiatus? *Nothing!* I need another nine months. God, take me back; this is too annoying and dramatic. I'm still attracted to the same bad-boy, moody, emotionally unhealthy guys I was before. When will it change? It wasn't supposed to be like this. I was supposed to be at some church social, see my Prince Charming across a crowded room, our eyes would meet, we'd talk and he'd compliment me on my deviled eggs, ask for my phone number, and that would be the start of my wonderful, honorable, Christian courtship. Then we'd live happily ever after, dancing in the kitchen of our beach house! And I'd have someone to sit with at church and attend couples events with on Valentine's Day. Why can't my life be like I plan? I like my plans. Why? Why? Why? Could someone explain it to me? If you created me like this, God, as a person who thrives in a controlled, well-thought-out environment, then why is my life so unplanned and chaotic?

What am I doing wrong and why do I go for the wrong guys and why do my emotions take over my brain the instant I see a great set of pecs and nice eyes? It just sort of happens this way. This guy probably doesn't even want to date me. He probably just likes to flirt with different women and that's it. That's cool. I just need to stay clear of his type, but old habits die hard, and I must be attracted to the challenge as much as he is attracted to the game. When will I learn, God? When will I learn? This is no longer amusing! I'm serious. I'm ready to grow up and date a real man by your standards. So where is he and how will I recognize him?

36

single and ranting

God, this sucks! All of a sudden I'm a restless child again, throwing temper tantrums in the car about what I want. I want ... I want ... I want ... to be loved, to be married, to control these raging hormones, these out-of-control emotional outbursts that make me think every cute guy I see in the grocery store could be my soul mate. I don't want to be that girl — the one who is always looking around in church searching for her husband. And I've been turning into that girl lately. And before this week I was doing so well — really. There was actually a point where I wasn't even thinking about men or dating; that was a peaceful, comfortable place. I think it lasted for about fifteen minutes.

I keep seeing my friends falling in love — meeting perfectly nice people on the internet. What's up with that? They fall in love, and I get a stalker?

I heard that you only give us what we can handle. So God, are you saying I can't handle a boyfriend right now? Am I so much more ill prepared for marriage than all of my friends who are married? What's the difference between them and me, except that I'm more vocal about the situation? I'm the one boycotting Valentine's Day and picketing all the candy and flower shops in solidarity with my non-valentine-having single sisters! I can't take this stuff lying down, and until I get a valentine, I think Hallmark should stop rubbing it in my face every February that I am alone!

I'm trying to wait on you, God—I really am—but it's been almost a whole year! A whole calendar year, which includes several major holidays without a date! Haven't I passed the test yet? I keep seeing these happy couples at church, and they've all come down different paths—some pretty scary—but you delivered them from their old selves and allowed them to find human love and affection and get married and take Sunday drives and have family picnics with their cute kids. When will it be my turn? Can I just have a clue? God, if I have these desires, aren't they natural and aren't they from you?

37

cheating on God

I have a few vices: sugar, email, Coca-Cola, carbohydrates, and Jewish men (not necessarily in that order). I have worked hard to overcome the latter. Seriously, there should be a support group for women like me.

I think my thing for Jewish men started when I fell for Corey Feldman in the movie *Goonies*. I think I was nine. He was the cute, funny one and most of the Jewish boys I've met since then have followed suit. Jewish men I've known are (a) charming, (b) they love their mothers, and (c) they value education highly, which makes them incredibly smart and witty. Many of them also *look* Italian with their dark hair and gorgeous brown eyes. (Since I'm Italian that's a plus in my family.) I realize I'm stereotyping to a certain degree, but this has been my personal experience.

The ones I like are usually about 5' 8" to 5' 9" and really well built. I never liked the Brad Pitts and the Ricky Schroeders growing up. I liked the Michael Rapaport and Patrick Dempsey types, the Woody Allens of my generation. It's like I have this thing my friends refer to as "Jewdar" … there can be a room full of a hundred eligible bachelors and I immediately zoom in on Ira Gershwitz and Justin Levinson! I just love them!

I've been dating Jewish men since I was eighteen. In fact, the college I attended was 30 percent Jewish and filled with New Yorkers. While living in New York City for a summer, my good buddy Evan Feldman took me out with ten of his funny, cute, charming friends, and I was smitten. I fell for one of them and we had a storybook New York summer romance. We walked in Central Park and did all the things I had seen in movies, so it was just perfect for me. I felt like I was in *When Harry Met Sally*. His name was Ryan and we've kept in touch for many years. We shared many things, but my biggest concern back then was finding a roommate in the sorority house that fall. So our little love affair of walks in Central Park ended amicably, and we went back to our separate colleges and became pen pals.

During my years at the University of Michigan, I spent many nights at the Jewish fraternity house, AEΠ. My little blonde sorority sisters and I couldn't get enough of those guys on — or off — the dance floor. One night I had a sassy *Dirty Dancing* reenactment with Avi Horowitz, trying to do that lift — you know, the one high in the air — and I ended up flat on my back. Avi ended up being a total flirt that night with me and my sorority sister Jen, whom he asked out as well.

I know generalizing men by religion may sound strange, but being Jewish is definitely a cultural thing, and there are so many beautiful things I love about it — the traditions, the ceremonies, and of course, the food. All the families of my Jewish boyfriends have been similar to my Italian family — warm, funny, and loving. Needless to say the Jewish mothers weren't exactly thrilled about them bringing me home with the possibility of them marrying "outside the faith."

During the time I was dating Steve, my Jewish love in Los Angeles, my mother made it quite clear that she was less than thrilled. I think her nagging actually kept us together longer. Stupid, I know, but I wanted to make my own choices. When we finally broke up, I waited over a month to tell her and saved it as a birthday present!

Okay, so I'm beyond all of that. As we know, I've been on the "boyfriend cleanse" for the past nine months. I went to New York City to see Evan and some other friends. Remember Rob, the born-again Christian from my musical theater program in college? Well, we met for a quick lunch in the park. Let's just say I can put any thoughts of a romance with him completely to rest. He's nice, but there were no sparks in any way, shape, or form. I knew the moment I saw him that this would be completely platonic. It's not like he didn't look great and act nicely—I just knew. No time to waste—whatsoever—moving on.

For a nice blonde from California, being in New York City is like being Alice in Wonderland. I kept seeing hot Jewish guys in suits—much different from seeing guys in wetsuits and board shorts. It was awesome. We're talking successful men with 401ks—very attractive!

One night during my stay with Evan, we went out to dinner with about twelve of our friends. Sitting across the table from me was this cute guy with a sweet smile. We couldn't talk much because it was so loud, but he was the perfect example of the charming, New York, Jewish man I've been describing. Joshua was sweet, shy, kinda funny, and adorable, with brown eyes, brown hair, wire-framed glasses, and shoulders and arms you just know are perfect for cuddling. (I always notice if a guy has nice shoulders.)

It was pouring rain as we ventured out after dinner. Josh offered me his arm as we walked and talked. We found out we went to the same college at the same time but never met. (A perfect cinematic beginning, right?) And we continued to talk at the next two bars. Our group seemed to be winding down around two in the morning, but I was wide awake and enjoying my conversations with Josh. I'm usually the first one to want to go home, but not this night!

As everyone else was leaving, we decided to burn the midnight oil and sit outside one of the cafés; we talked and talked until we were asked to leave at three o'clock. Josh had traveled the world and was extremely intelligent. He also had a gentle spirit and listened intently to what I had to share. We talked about God, my story, his beliefs, my beliefs, life, and relationships—past and present. He was so intelligent and cultured and well read on every subject. I was fascinated by his experiences and vice versa. It was so nice to connect and to be totally open with a stranger, yet feel so comfortable. It was a special connection, but for the first time in my life, I wasn't getting caught up in emotions. I was truly in the moment and enjoying everything we had to say. (Honest! I'm not lying.) We walked many blocks together and kept sharing stories and theories. It was the kind of night you'd see in a movie, but this was really happening. Two people meet, make a connection, and time seems to stand still. At one point, Josh referred to a quote by Albert Einstein: "When you're with someone you really like, every hour seems like a minute." How true.

When we arrived at his neighborhood, it was about four in the morning. He was so sweet and neither of us was looking for anything physical or romantic. It was weird! We both realized that besides geographical distance, we had some religious differences that would not allow us to pursue a relationship. So that was that.

For a brief moment I felt like I had escaped my California life. I'm usually so into the entertainment industry or the beach and just being casual. It's sort of a Blockbuster movie-renting, beach-barbecue kind of life. That night we talked about poetry, great books we had read, and his gourmet French cooking. He's a total New Yorker. It was exciting and fun. He casually asked if I wanted to continue this conversation at another diner or go upstairs, and I didn't even think anything of it. (Besides, Evan's air conditioner was broken and it was a hot summer night. I did have some ulterior motives.) We went up to his apartment, and he sat me down in a chair and propped my feet up and read to me. He had the made-for-TV New York City apartment—small with high ceilings and lots and lots of books. We listened to jazz and read poetry from Pablo Neruda until the sun came up. He was so excited about sharing these things with me; he was like a little kid and I found it absolutely charming. Even at five o'clock, as tired as we both were, we didn't want this night to end.

Here's the trashy part ... I asked if I could stay at his place until the next morning, which it already was. So what was the harm? I'm a grown woman and I can handle this, right? Besides, there hadn't been one bit of flirting, or even my typical sarcastic banter the whole night! We ended up talking and I drifted off to sleep around 9:30 a.m.

It was wonderful, romantic, and special. He said some of the sweetest things I had ever heard. We discovered that we did have romantic feelings for each other, but we had fought the urge to act on them. He knew my whole theory about waiting on God and saving myself physically and emotionally for marriage. I knew my stance and he knew mine, but let's just say I bent the rules a little bit that night—or I fell off the wagon of purity I'd been on for the past nine months. The emotions inside of me were too strong and I was too weak; I had put myself in a tempting situation and I knew better, yet I didn't care. I allowed the romance between us to take over and I fully embraced it (well, not fully, but you get the picture).

Let's get something straight for my mother's sake: I'm not saying this was a physical encounter that would make me appear cheap. The fact was I didn't get in a cab and go home; I stayed and let things go to that next level. It was an intensity I hadn't planned on experiencing unless the relationship was leading to marriage. I'm no expert on "Christian boundaries," so all I can say is I know I crossed some!

I was done with these spontaneous affairs of the heart ... done with the intense dramas that started out this way and ended in despair. I was grown-up ... or so I thought. We saw each other again on Sunday night, and it was one of those perfect evenings I only see in depressing chick flicks—but it was real and it was happening to me. We walked and had dinner at this perfect little place with outside seating and ivy covered walls, sat, and talked and talked. He held my hand across the table, and I lost my train of thought. He listened intently to everything I had to say; he had this way of making me feel like I was the most important person in the world. He complemented me in so many ways. I caught myself secretly saying to God: "I know I don't deserve it, but is there any possible way you could reveal yourself to this man? Right now, perhaps? Plleeeease?"

I know it's crazy, but I was falling for Joshua and couldn't help myself. He was making it very hard for me to want to go back to Los Angeles and have feelings for anyone else. All my boyfriend-fasting went completely down the drain. Like many women, I had emotionally committed myself to a stranger after only a short period of time. I knew exactly what I was doing and how hard it would be to leave him. He had all the qualities of someone I'd like to date except one—the most important one. As he put it, when everyone was standing at the station and the "Jesus train" came by, he didn't get on it. This Christianity thing was one of our staple topics for the remainder of my visit. I gave it my best shot, and I must say I had a captive audience in Joshua. He was fascinated with my life, my faith, my choices. He had no idea how off-the-wagon I had fallen in my own mind.

After two wonderful nights, our time was over and I was on a plane back to Los Angeles. He mentioned flying out to see me the next month, but I didn't think there were any real intentions behind that suggestion. He and I both logically knew this couldn't go any further, even though we were kind of avoiding the inevitable. Of course I wanted him to come to Los Angeles, and he even mentioned going to church with me. Why did he even have to say that and give me a glimmer of hope? It's too hard to go there and I can't do the missionary-dating thing. Or can I? No, the Bible says not to be unequally yoked, right? So that covers this topic. Why can't I get it through my head?

I'd only been back in LA a few days, and I hadn't prayed to God much because I felt guilty for my actions ... well, I sort of felt guilty. I knew part of it was wrong, biblically speaking, but why didn't it feel wrong? It did to a degree and it's like I'd been avoiding talking to

God for fear of his disapproval and discipline. What *was* he thinking? I wished he would talk to me and reveal what was wrong or right. If everything is predestined in our lives, did God put Joshua in my life for a reason? If so, what was it? Was I supposed to be a witness to him? And if so, why did I blow it? Did I cheat on God that weekend by focusing all my attention on a man and not on him? I was confused; this was all so new for me. If this had happened to me a couple of years before, there would *not* have been any guilt. I'm going to just chalk it up to my life being like the movies and call it a day!

So I'm thinking maybe I'm not cut out for this old-fashioned courting I've been told about. I'm obviously too weak to control myself, at least right now. So what's the solution? Become a nun? Wait another nine months? Will I ever get it right? It's just another example of life turning out completely different than I planned or prepared for. Josh showed me some valuable things. He reminded me of the way I want and deserve to be treated by a man, and that I shouldn't settle for anything less than goose bumps. What happened from there I just didn't know.

38

joshua

When I returned home to California, a dozen roses and a sweet poetic card were waiting for me. Three days later Joshua booked a plane ticket to come visit. At this point my life was back in the movies, just the way I like it—dramatic and thrilling. As my friend Karen says, "Kerri, you love the long shot. You're a hopeless romantic." She's right.

Well, the plan was to have him come to church so he could get converted and we would live happily ever after in my beach house, cooking great meals, laughing, dancing in the kitchen, and reading poetry and great literature. But I was still worried about what had happened in New York. I repented to God for my sins after beating myself up with guilt for several days. I felt like a little girl that had been bad, and I didn't want to go see my Father because I knew I'd be in trouble. It took me several days before I could even talk to God about it. I know that's not the way he wanted it; I just had all this Catholic guilt to deal with.

It took some serious time for me to feel like I was worthy to be a Christian again, even though I know God doesn't feel that way. He forgives me and instantly forgets my slipups. So why couldn't I forgive myself? Life was easier in a way when I was blinded and could do so many things in ignorance, not feeling any guilt. Guilt is a weapon Satan uses to keep us down, depressed, and unproductive! We have no power when we are imprisoned in guilt and condemnation. It's a battle to accept that when we give our lives to the Lord we are free from the yoke of our past transgressions and the ones to come.

Joshua and I talked on the phone every day. The conversations we had were flirtatious at times and serious at times. We talked about our different religions. I would get emails from him with questions about my faith. I even sent him a book on Christianity in hopes that he would read it and have God's truth revealed. At first I just wanted to see Josh get saved so I could date him, but over time as I grew to care about him, I wanted his salvation to come for his sake and not mine — well, most of the time.

I wanted him to understand that indescribable peace and joy that I have. I remember a guy back in college who was a Christian and he was so happy all the time. It seemed as though he wanted us all to be like him, so I asked him why. He said, "It's like I found the most amazing pizza, and I just want to share it with all my friends." I thought he was nuts at the time, but now I get it.

The day arrived for Joshua's visit, and I went to pick him up at the airport, bound and determined to be the ultimate Christian witness. I'd win his heart over to me and my team if it was the last thing I did.

Well, I was a good witness — for about half a day. I told him he couldn't even hold my hand since we were "just friends." He was so sweet, good-looking, charming, and funny. He bought me fresh flowers. Who does that? We walked on the beach, we laughed and talked. Within hours I knew it was game over. There was already an emotional connection from the emails and late-night phone calls.

I broke down to him the first night he was in town and told him I knew this whole situation was going to get messy. He didn't believe me — he wanted to live for the moment — but he was respectful of my wishes.

I was advised by my mentor and all my Christian friends not to have him stay at my apartment, but I was determined to be strong and overcome any temptation. And where else would he have stayed? I couldn't ask him to pay for a hotel, right? That would be weird, I thought. We even discussed all my boundaries beforehand. But it was like walking right into a fire and not expecting to get burned.

During the next seven days, Josh and I enjoyed every moment together. He fell in love with California and I fell in love with him—or something like it. He surfed, we went to the beach, we had parties with friends, he cooked gourmet meals for me and my friends, we went to my church and he liked it. I even hiked for him! It must have been love or insanity. I don't hike. I don't even sweat if I can help it! My mother always said, "If God had intended for us to hike, he wouldn't have invented valet parking!"

It was a running joke between us all week about him converting, leaving New York, and coming out here to live happily ever after. "Joshua, you're two more holidays away from 'happily ever after,' honey! And I can make great latkes and celebrate all the existing holidays with you." We had some great conversations on the subject of how we could make it work. The thing is, we both started to buy into the fantasy. Except in his fantasy, he would be wearing a yarmulke and we would be lighting the menorah instead of a Christmas tree. I still held out hope. God could do a miracle—and this was such a small one.

Joshua seemed to love everyone at my church picnic; he even entered the pie-eating contest. I had introduced him to all my friends as my "Jewish love who was about to convert and marry me." We were funny together and people enjoyed our routines. He even had long talks with guys from my church. People were definitely working hard for me.

He made me feel beautiful, appreciated, and validated in all the ways I'd been yearning for. He would say the kind of things you hear in movies and actually mean them. We were both smitten for sure. It had been ten months since I had broken up with my ex of two years. I was off hiatus and back in the saddle. Something felt so right about it, and yet deep down inside something felt so wrong. I had an instant boyfriend and he was crazy about me! The unsettling part was that my behavior was so wrong. I had taken matters into my own hands and had forgotten about waiting on God. I found this guy and was bound and determined to make it work—on *my* terms, not God's. I mean, he had all—well, all but one—of the qualities I'd been looking for in a man.

When I was with Joshua, everything was giddy and funny and life seemed satisfying. But I had gone against everything I believed in and had been preaching to others about for months. I mean, I was the poster child for waiting on God and now look at me ... falling right back into my emotional and controlling ways, manufacturing this relationship to fulfill my needs. I was leading a Bible study, for goodness' sake, filled with single Christian girls that looked up to me and my choices! What a hypocrite I had become; they always say pride comes before the fall.

Why couldn't God overlook the fact that we were totally in sin with our behavior on most levels? Joshua mentioned that his family would disown him if he became a Christian; he had been programmed his whole life with the Jewish culture and the idea that Christians and Jews don't mix. Actually, it was more than that; he had been told that Christians didn't even like Jews.

So let's cut to the chase. We had a wonderful week together, and I totally ignored my moral codes, gave in to my desires, and gave my heart to him. I didn't really see it happening. I thought I was in control. Ha! When he told me he was coming to California, I thought, *Wow, another chance to be a good witness.* What a joke! A witness to what?

I'd been praying for months for a God-centered relationship, built on biblical principles, including purity. With this one I thought I could do it backward—pick the guy myself, try to add the godly principles, and then ask God to bless it—just like I did with Jake—except God wasn't laughing this time. He knew I was going to get hurt; there was no way around it.

After a tearful, dramatic, goofy goodbye, and many Norah Jones songs on the car radio on the way to the airport, I pulled myself together as I walked to my car. Josh had filled my tank with gas and even left money for the parking. He was so perfect, and I was so smitten. He seemed the type to really meet my needs on most levels. Had I traded in a guy who prays for a guy who cooks? As sexy as a man making a dinner is, the thought of a man praying for me or with me blows that out of the water! Well, so I've been told. I had never really experienced much praying with my boyfriends. I guess I forgot that part.

So the next day Josh called about five times and the day after that and the day after that. "This hurts," he said. "I never knew I could fall so hard." I wanted to say, "I told you this would suck," but I refrained. I was comforted to know he was miserable too. Am I so mature or what? So once again the saga continued—over emails and the phone. He continued to make me laugh and our bond kept growing more intimate. We talked about God a lot, so I was able to rationalize my behavior. Besides, I was the only Christian he knew personally. I know it sounds crazy, but remember—he's from New York. I just kept sending him more books!

After Josh left, once again my good friends "guilt" and "condemnation" came for a visit. Funny how much in denial I was when he was here. "Carpe Diem"—live for the moment, Kerri! It wasn't worth it for the amount of pain I felt afterward.

I'm learning not to place myself in tempting situations and expect to be able to miraculously resist. That's just dumb! We're only human and I don't care how strong I think I am, emotions are powerful things—they can rationalize almost any behavior—for the moment. But it won't last.

So as Josh and I kept emailing and talking, our conversations were very intense at times—"Danger, Will Robinson, danger!" Be careful what you say and hear in these types of situations; you'll start to buy into the fantasy. We joked about our life together, and we confessed that we made each other feel things that we hadn't felt in a long time. I feed off that stuff—he's a charming guy telling me I'm amazing and the kind of woman he wants to marry. He just said it would be a long game of "religious chicken," and we would see who would cave in first. I was game; I knew he would come around—even if it was just to be with me. I didn't care as long as he got there. I knew he'd give his heart to the Lord. Guess what? It didn't happen.

39

waiting on God ...
proactively

As Josh and I were playing this waiting game, I finally decided to go on a date with Elliot, a sweet one from the internet. We had been emailing for nine months now and had exchanged pictures and even knew the same people. I felt like this could be the perfect way to transition into my new lifestyle with a Christian boyfriend and get over pining for Josh.

The day arrived for the big date and Elliot showed up at my door dressed very nicely and looking quite attractive. I was pumped. We chatted during dinner. Sushi — a nice start. And that is all it was. By 6:45 I knew this guy had no chance whatsoever. Actually, I knew at about 6:15, five minutes after he picked me up, but I was trying to be open.

We took a walk on the beach. It was 7:15 p.m., it was cold, and I wanted to go home. I was bored to tears! Why? I don't know. Oh right, I do know. It's because this guy was local, totally loved the Lord, attractive, had a good job, and was interested in me. But even though he had a great physique and a nice smile, he was sooo boring! I was dying! He made several attempts at being funny, but it was piti-ful. I don't mean to be rude, but it was just plain sad.

In reality, we had no chemistry; I can't tell you why. My friends believe in the three-date rule before moving on, but I'm not into that. If I know, I know ... and I knew he wasn't for me. Why would I want that? I came home depressed. "What's wrong with me?" I thought. "Why can't I find a Christian who makes me laugh?"

Elliot was so not funny or intellectually stimulating. We didn't click at all. The only thing we had in common was the Lord. He picked me up at six o'clock and at about seven thirty I found myself giving the "Wow! It's getting late" speech. The funny thing about dates like this one — the guy doesn't get the hint I'm putting out there; he thinks it's going amazingly well, especially after he whipped out his flash cards of all the engineering terms he was learning for work! Oh be still my beating heart! ARRRGH! He even asked me out again right there. Did he not know I was trying to blow him off? Do we girls need a sign? "This is not going to happen again! Don't call me!" It was over.

After the date, people kept saying, "Give it some time, Kerri." Well, that never works for me. I know if I can picture myself with someone or not, right away. It's chemistry and I can't manufacture it. If I could, I'd bottle it and make a million dollars!

I was stuck. I was still holding out for a miracle from Josh with no sign of anything happening, except our bond getting stronger and our phone bills getting larger. And then it hit me. I lost it. I was this close to going to New York. He kept inviting me, and I had a layover there on a trip I was planning. Even though I promised my-self I would never do that, I was about to, and this was a huge reality check. I rationalized it at first — that it would only be one night and surely I could keep it together for one night. Besides, it would be the day before my birthday, and I wanted to feel special on my birthday! What's the big deal?

I told Trista, my confidant, what I was about to do, and she cau-tioned me and told me to pray about it. She asked me if I heard God's voice in all of this. I said, "Shut up! Don't bring him into this. Okay, so no! I haven't heard anything, so I assumed it was okay." Ya think it was because I wasn't listening?

I couldn't see that I might have been ignoring his gentle nudging to break these bonds and get my heart back where it belonged—with him. God wanted my heart back. And I didn't even want to pray about going to New York City. I just prayed for Josh to get saved; I had a one-track mind. I even quoted Mark 11:24—"I tell you, whatever you ask for in prayer, believe that you have received it, and it will be yours." I was all over that verse every day. I mean I prayed, "God, you parted the Red Sea. Can't you do me this one little favor?"

One night I was talking with Josh about coming to New York. I told him it was a big deal to me and had caused me to reevaluate exactly what we were doing. Reality time. He said, "Well, Kerri, you want to settle down with a Christian guy. I'm not that guy and never will be that guy." That was like a knife cutting through my heart. I was stunned and hurt.

Then I told him to stop calling me every day. We had a discussion about what we both wanted and it was clear: At that moment we had no future. I couldn't let go, though I knew I had to. He wanted to keep me in his life and try to transition into being just friends. Friends! What? *That* would be impossible and we both knew it. I was so hurt! How could he even think of wanting to be just friends after everything he'd told me? If I was *so* amazing that I rocked his world, wouldn't he do anything to have me? I just wanted the happy ending.

I went to Trista's and asked her to pray for me. She prayed that the bonds between Josh and me would be broken. As she prayed, I felt a peace come over me. I knew I was doing God's will, but that night was still awful. I hung out with my good Jewish hottie friend, Junx, and ate Mexican food, but that didn't cheer me up. I had the breakup blues. I was in so much pain. I had a lot of healing to do and I had to do it without Josh in my life.

I went to church the next day and prayed again with Cathy who is in leadership and also a prayer warrior for me. I tell her she's cheaper than therapy. I just call it being "discipled." I told her everything and she prayed to God to help me get back up after falling. She thanked him that I was completely forgiven. She told me I shouldn't be talking to Josh and that I should lay this whole situation at the foot of the cross and let God handle Josh's salvation. But that was so hard, because I wanted to help God—like he needs it, right?

Cathy reminded me that God understands my desire to be loved and cherished, and also to be married, but I had to wait on his timing. I just still couldn't believe I had let this happen to me after so many months of being okay with being alone!

So here's what I'm learning: Anyone can fall ... and it can happen fast! Don't have so much pride as to think you're invincible because you're not. I wasn't.

I was okay during the church service. After the sermon the praise band played one more song, and our worship leader said, "Don't leave here today until God is done with you." The band proceeded to play a beautiful song about making God your love and how we may be lost, but he finds us. One of the lyrics spoke right to my heart: "I'm undone and I dare not move / Love has found me." I was finally broken. I fell to my knees and the tears came and would not stop. I felt forgiven and overwhelmed with God's goodness. As I was crying out to him, I knew I heard his voice: "I've got you, Kerri, right here in my arms, and I won't let you go." How could I have forsaken that kind of love?

God didn't let me go to New York and he didn't let me stray too far. I'm so beyond grateful for that and for everything my heavenly Father is to me. Even when I'm trying to run the show, he's there, patiently waiting for me to give back his spot in the director's chair.

I talked to Joshua one last time. I was bold and even read some passages to him about Jesus, straight from the Bible. He respects me but thinks I'm crazy for wanting him to convert to Christianity. To him that means abandoning his Jewish identity and his entire family.

I tried to explain that Christians are just fulfilled Jews with two more major holidays. "And besides," I added, "ham tastes good!"

I told Josh I needed to heal my heart, and we couldn't talk for awhile. He didn't really think I'd stick to it. And why should he? I had compromised on other things I said I wouldn't do. I didn't have a very good track record! So he called me the next day but I didn't call back. Another night he called twice; one time I answered and explained that I needed space and time. He was annoyed. He didn't want to stop talking; he just wanted to transition to being friends. Ha! Like it's that easy! I told him I'd be praying for him; he was not impressed. I felt terrible and I wanted to call him back or email him. I even dialed most of his phone number once but resisted at the last minute—thanks to the strength God gave me.

So another one bites the dust, and I'm back to the drawing board. I think that's where God likes me, at least for now. I want to get back to that place of rest where I was a few months ago. I didn't need anyone but God; he was my love affair and I miss that peace.

40

last call

Josh called me Sunday night. I told him I'd be there if he ever really needed me. It had been eight days since we last talked. He had dinner with some friends at this place where he took me in New York. He was sad. After we hung up, I felt sad. The next morning he was on my mind again. Ugh!

I was doing so well, and then when we talked, it was like opening Pandora's box. I wanted to email him, but he beat me to it. A couple of days went by and then he called again. I told him he couldn't call me, that it was too hard right now. He was being selfish because he just wanted me in his life. He wanted to be friends. Well, we didn't start out that way, and it was almost impossible to go back. I don't know if it's possible. We'll see.

I guess Josh made me feel lonely again—realizing I don't have that "last phone call" of the night any longer. Everyone around me seems to have that someone they can rely on to tell their secret hopes and dreams to, and all I have is my stuffed Winnie the Pooh. He's a great listener but doesn't really talk back much. Seriously, it's so painful knowing that I might have had a sample with Joshua of what "great love" is, and now it's been yanked away from me. Maybe I don't know what true love is in God's eyes? I doubt I've ever experienced it or I would be married by now. I think it's deeper than great poetry and long walks on the beach. It must have something to do with commitment when things get ugly and giving more of yourself to the other person than you could ever imagine. I've seen great love and not just in movies, and I know in my heart God has that for me. It may be a long time before I get it, but I think I need to concentrate on being content with God giving me everything I need for right now. But I'm telling you, it's so hard!

God will heal me, I know; it just takes time. It's funny how we can still feel saddened in the midst of all the blessings in our lives. I have so much to be thankful for.

dear God

Dear God,

I'm trying to make my time with you a priority—I really am and I'm doing a lousy job and I don't even have kids to blame it on. I feel so busy, busy, busy, but it's all so stressful, and I just have trouble sitting still long enough to talk with you. As you know, writing my feelings down helps me because it slows my thoughts and lets me focus. Help me, Father. I'm your daughter, asking for discipline and patience in my life.

Today I got up and went to yoga, came home, checked my "To Do" list and started cleaning, did some email and phone calls, and ran around my apartment. I don't even like yoga, but I thought I needed something to calm me down. It didn't work. I kept laughing at everyone moaning and groaning and chanting! You had to be laughing too, weren't you?

My intentions were to wake up, spend some time in prayer and in your Word. That probably would have been better than the yoga for me, huh?

Why is that so hard for me? I'm so grateful for your patience, God, and the grace you give me to start all over again tomorrow.

I love you,
Kerri

Dear God,

Okay, what can I say? I thought falling off the wagon with Josh was bad but I hit another all-time low today—really! Do I dare write about it? I got back on that darned chatroom! I know! I know it's insane, and you are not happy. I don't know what got into me after everything I've been through. I really feel like it's a bad addiction, and once I signed on that stupid thing and started browsing through all these seemingly normal Christian profiles, I was hooked. I'm just so sick of seeing all my friends going on match.com, *or whatever, and then finding true love. Even the Christian radio stations are advertising these websites! What's a girl to do? Wait … Wait … That's all I keep hearing in my prayers, but I just can't seem to master the "art of waiting."*

Love,
Kerri

Dear God in heaven,

I'm sick of waiting. I'm not trying to be disrespectful or make light of this, God. I'm just being real. I'm tired of being alone; it sucks right now. I'm not sugarcoating it, and I know I'm supposed to be walking around with a happy face, saying how content I am being single. But God, I don't feel content. I feel anxious, and please forgive me for not being patient. But why do some people get to be proactive and some don't? I'm confused. I know perfectly normal Christians that have gone online, and then I go on and get a stalker and a series of other unfortunate experiences—none of which have been fruitful in any way! What is wrong with me?

Love,
Kerri

42

women's lib is bringing me down!

I'm sick of hearing all this: "I don't need a man! I'm fine! I'm a self-sufficient woman of the new millennium!" Okay, that's crap! I need a man and I'm not afraid to say it. There are important times in a woman's life when having a man around would be useful, such as when you are unloading heavy luggage. I needed a man desperately when I decided to purchase a 150-pound hammock today at Costco. I knew I couldn't lift that box into my car, much less get it up the stairs into my apartment.

Half of my lifelong dream of owning a beach house and a hammock was about to come true. I asked the store manager if someone would help me to my car. I *had* to buy it then—it was on sale. He said, "Sure. This gentleman will help you." Right before my eyes was Derek. "Well hellooo, Derek, you tall drink of water, you!" (Okay, I didn't say that out loud ... or did I?) Derek was *hot* in that really-well-built-I-lift-boxes-for-a-living way. And he had that all-American smile and really nice eyes.

Was I imagining this? It had been a long time since I found someone attractive that worked in a public place. I looked again. He was definitely hot! We chatted a bit and he loaded my new purchase into the cart. I found out Mr. Derek was working two jobs while putting himself through school. Very nice.

I made my usual small talk as I silently prayed, "Dear God, please help me out here. How forward can I be? Is he going to ask me out or what?" It had been so long; I had lost my game. Thoughts of "waiting on God" occurred to me, but I quickly brushed them aside.

An opportunity had presented itself and I had two goals: (1) Get him to ask me out, and (2) Get someone to help me carry this stupid box up to my apartment.

We walked out to the car and he casually joked, "You know, my truck is over there if it doesn't fit into your car." "Okay, let's go!" I said playfully in that I'm-half-serious kinda way. *Let the games begin*, I thought. He likes me ... or does he? He could just be bored. I mean, how many chances does he get at Costco to flirt with women? Hmmm ... I wonder what the benefits of dating him would be? A free membership? That could be good.

But he did take about ten minutes to get the hammock loaded in my trunk because I pretended not to know how to fold the seats down. This ordeal was a bit humiliating because my trunk was a mess. It contained everything from my circa 1970s tennis shoe roller skates, to a badminton set and some old jeans. But most importantly, my trunk contained about fifty — I kid you not — Joyce Meyer ministry tapes. He picked one up and said, "*Let God Be God*, huh?" "Yeah, those are my Christian ministry tapes." (Just putting it out there.) "Right on," he smiled. That's all I got. I didn't know if it was "Right on! I'm into that too" or "Right on ... just right on!" I didn't push it. Plenty of time for that later. Back to work!

As our time together ended, I wasn't any closer to my goal. I had only received mild flirtations. I had to act fast. He finally says to me, "Well, Kerri, when you come back, if you ever need anything, I'll be here." That was not good enough. I blurted out as he was about to walk away, "Do you like comedy?" "Yes," he said. "Well, do you want to come see some? Of me, I mean?" "You're a comedienne? I should have guessed by your shoes," he said pointing to my hot pink Converses paired with my khaki dress pants, blouse, and pearls. I quickly pulled out my card, wrote my email address, and told him to email me and I'd invite him to my shows. He seemed excited. He said, "I'll definitely shoot you an email and sign it 'Costco Guy.'" I made my last feeble attempt: "Yeah, and maybe I could get some help lifting some heavy furniture at my house sometime." "Most definitely!" he replied. Score for Kerri! Well, kinda. The stupid box was still hanging out of my trunk.

I called my friends Trista, Suz, and Gina and repeated the whole story word for word ... mainly for comic effect. They laughed at me. So what else is new? They get joy from my humiliation.

Later in the afternoon, I was faced with the prospect of unloading the stupid hammock myself. I was on a time clock because I had an appointment and couldn't keep the box hanging out of my trunk any longer. I got a knife and decided to do it piece-by-piece (my friend Barry's suggestion). Well, the first piece was made of iron and weighed about fifty pounds. I tried to think of myself as this self-sufficient woman, but come on! I was sweating, and that goes against everything I stand for as a woman with a southern upbringing! This was a nightmare. I resisted the urge to sit on the curb and cry. I wanted my hammock, but was I willing to go through all this? Each piece was heavier than the last. At one point a man walked up and offered to help. He helped with the biggest piece and I thanked him profusely. It turned out he lived in my building with his lovely wife and child. Of course! Prince Charming is never single!

I finished the daunting task, and it put me in a really bad mood. I didn't feel any sense of accomplishment. I felt dirty and sweaty, and that is just wrong. The phone rang. "Hey there! What are ya doin?" "Uuugh!" I cried. "Where are you when I need you?" "Missouri," a sweetly familiar voice uttered. It was Todd Kramer calling to check in. He does that from time to time; we catch up and I'm reminded that he's happily married to that bikini model. Alas! Even Todd was not able to cheer me up. Oh well. I made it to Pilates class on time, but I wasn't happy.

The day ended with Mexican food and a movie night with my girls. All in all, I'm glad it's over. And when I'm sipping lemonade and lounging in my hammock as I listen to the ocean breeze, I'll laugh about all this. But not one minute before!

43

enter mr. h.

Okay, so enter stage right—Bachelor Number Twenty-one, Mr. H. The *H* stands for "hottie" and he is definitely my type. He has a preppy style and wears clothes from Banana Republic and Ralph Lauren. He has broad shoulders, a devilish smile, and the kind of blue eyes that seem to look right through you, plus long lashes. When I look at him, there always seems to be something going on behind his eyes; it intrigues me to find out what this guy is all about. Other girls would find him really cute, so he falls into the category I usually like because he'd be great at parties. I know this is immature, but I'm just being honest with you. It's very high school and someday I'll get over it. Or will I? Sometimes when you meet a guy there is something alluring and you can't put your finger on it, but you know it's there ... dare I say seduction? I guess I'll call it attraction or chemistry. I'm big on instant chemistry, you know. I always expect the music to play in the background when a new character enters the scene and, yes, the band is playing that old familiar song. And I'm about to start the dance again!

I met Mr. H. at a Hollywood function and was immediately attracted to him. He's an actor. I know, I know ... "Danger, Will Robinson, danger!" But he's so darn hot! We started flirting in that sarcastic way I revert to when I'm nervous. He's also from the South and has this twinge of the sexiest southern drawl you've ever heard. He's Christian—to what extent I'm not sure—and most importantly, he makes me laugh. He's very funny in that sarcastic way that I love so much. Is that healthy? Probably not, but who cares? Mr. H. and I talked about movies and sports and he said, "Well, why don't I invite you over to watch the football game on Saturday and cook you breakfast?" Smooth ... very smooth. This way he wasn't committing to a date; just something more casual where we could "hang out" and he could see if I was worth him paying for dinner! I was on to him. I told him to call me. He flaked out that first week and didn't call.

He finally did end up calling me out of the blue one day, and after that we started talking on the phone every few days. I invited him to join me at a party in Hollywood one Saturday night but he didn't show. I actually called him on my way home to ask what his deal was. (Yes, I broke the cardinal rule of being the strong powerful woman that I am by calling.) We were talking and I'm halfway back to the beach at this point (he lives on the other side of Hollywood). In that slow, sultry, southern voice, he asks, "What are you doing right now?" Uh ... I knew this was a trick question. Did he actually want to see me? It was twelve thirty at night and my bedtime was two hours ago. "I'm ... um ... driving ... um ... around ..."

Mr. H.: Want to meet up?

Kerri: Uh ... what, now? Tonight?

Mr. H.: Yeah ... why not? Where are you?

Kerri: Not far from Hollywood. (Lie: I'm halfway home.)

Mr. H.: Great! Meet me at Lola's in thirty minutes! Can't wait to see ya darling.

Kerri: Yeah ... sure ... make sure you show up this time!

So now our heroine is turning the car around in full throttle and busting it all the way back to Hollywood to meet some guy who has stood her up twice now! Well, he didn't actually stand me up, but his track record has shown him to be either flaky or a total player.

So we met at one o'clock for Cokes in a trendy Hollywood hot spot, and I couldn't help thinking this is where I used to go with Jake, my ex that I dated for two years … the other bad boy! When will I learn? This place was okay, but I wasn't into "that scene" anymore, and I could tell Mr. H. was right at home there. We had great conversation and actually talked seriously for a bit. He walked me out to my car and I invited him to come see me in a show that coming weekend on Sunday night. He said he'd try to make it. The next morning I was so tired I could barely stay awake, but it made for a great story to my girlfriends of how fun and spontaneous I was! I'm always about a great story!

So what do you know? Mr. H. didn't make it to my show that Sunday. And guess what I did? I actually called this guy myself *again* on the phone! I just had the attitude of "I don't care about rules anymore and I'll call who I want, when I want! I'm not twenty-two anymore!" That's right, but I was acting like a desperate teenager. He said he had to go to Sunday night "church" and he couldn't skip it. He apologized and then started making jokes. We talked forever that night.

After that he would call me almost every day. Our conversations would last for hours and consist of 25 percent serious and 75 percent making fun of one another with witty repartee. He can more than keep up with me when it comes to that stuff, but it's exhausting—even for me. I think I like this kind of joking because it shows me that a guy has a quick wit. The sarcasm usually comes with a sense of confidence, or should I say cockiness, that for some reason appeals to me. Why is it that I like the guys that seem so untamed and challenging?

I kept thinking, *Be careful what you wish for,* because I wanted someone funny and I got it, but how far can the sarcasm go? When we talked, it was like a tennis match and we kept one-upping each other. It's all innocent fun; I've never been offended. It just reminds me of two school kids trying to keep the upper hand.

Why am I like this? He's definitely someone I'd enjoy getting to know, but I keep myself so guarded by joking. He even said to me one night, "Oh, Kerri, you just don't want me to know you like me because you think I'll have the upper hand and you don't want to feel vulnerable." I said, "That's ridiculous and this isn't a game, silly." But I think he hit the nail on the head. I don't want to feel vulnerable again because then I can get hurt. With Josh it was so unplanned. With him being in New York, it was more fantasy than reality. Plus, we had such an instant romantic connection the first night we met; there were no games; we just let our emotions take over and started acting all cheesy right away. That is because we didn't take anything slowly—my typical pattern.

For once I'd like to guard my heart. I'd like a guy to get to know me without the skewed vision that new romance brings. In the past, I've gotten so close, so fast, that objectivity was out the window, much less seeking God's opinion. I had a one-track mind in past relationships, and I'd like to think God has helped me grow and learn from my mistakes. I'm just not too sure he's thrilled with the way I'm handling this one.

So now Mr. H. is in my life and is expressing interest in me, and I'm looking for reasons to be dramatic. He told me jokingly, "In your search for perfection, you're looking for flaws in me so you can bolt." That unfortunately wasn't far from the truth. We ladies say we want a relationship so badly, but when one comes our way, we look for reasons not to get involved. Putting yourself out there can be risky. We risk rejection; we risk getting hurt or hurting someone else. I don't think that is the way God intends us to feel. I think he wants us to stay focused on him and realize he is the only thing in our entire lives that is not going to disappoint or hurt us. Humans fail; men fail. There is no perfect guy, only the perfect choice God has for us.

I have no idea what that picture is going to look like. I can hope and pray and try to plan it all out in my mind, but like everything else in life, it won't be that way. It never is. It's better if it's God's will. I'm just so set on doing this right for once, and it's about time I did!

But what does "right" mean? We know there aren't any rules of courtship and dating in the Bible, so what do we do? Well, after I get done worrying and obsessing—old pattern and still working on it—I pray. I ask others to pray for me. I tell God I don't want to go one day longer than he ordains. He knows my heart; he knows I have the best intentions. He also knows I'm weak and can easily get swept away by the notion of romance. So I'm trying to stay focused on God. I'm getting to know Mr. H. and doing my best to see him objectively—which is not easy. I'm learning as I go, but I'm guarding my heart so if God tells me this is not the man for me, I won't be devastated. I have to throw out my checklist anyway because nobody's perfect and anyone can fail. That doesn't mean I head for the door. Or does it?

44

is it supposed to feel like this?

Okay, so I'm starting to really like Mr. H. He's a Christian, and it's everything I wanted in theory, except now I have that nauseous feeling in my stomach. Some would call it butterflies; I call it annoying. I find myself checking too many times to see if he called.

God is so faithful. As I was driving around today, fixating on this new man in my life and wondering why he didn't call last night, God gently spoke to me. This doesn't happen often in my life, but when it does it comes with crystal clarity. He said to me, "My dear Kerri, why are you sad? You don't hear from this man for one day. You barely know him. He didn't even matter to you two weeks ago. He's done nothing for you yet, but you are giving him all this attention. I've been with you your whole life and given you everything. Now you know how sad I get, Kerri, when you go about your day and I don't hear from you. I want you to long to hear from me!" That hit me right in the heart, and I literally had to stop the car.

It was so clear that God felt neglected because I'd been taking him for granted. I do that when things are good. It's when I've screwed things up that I turn to God—most times. But wow! He is so patient, loving, and full of grace ... and I'm *not*! I have no grace. It's like I have this picture of how things should be done, and when someone veers to the left of my plan I'm annoyed to say the least. I don't lean on God. I don't make God my rock. I lean on my own rules, plans, and theories. Well, guess what? Those are all bound to fail at some point, and God never fails me! Never!

"The LORD is my light and my salvation — whom shall I fear? The LORD is the stronghold of my life — of whom shall I be afraid?" (Psalm 27:1). If he is *truly* in control of my life and my relationships, why do I need to stress over a stupid phone call?

45

practice what you preach

Now that there's a guy in the picture, I'm trying to actually apply some of these principles I've been writing about. Waiting—waiting is good; waiting is hard. I stopped calling Mr. H. and I'm letting him initiate when we see each other. That's good, right? I'm not any more patient than I was a couple years ago. I thought taking all this time off from dating and spending it with the Lord would make me stronger and more centered when the next guy came along. But I don't feel stronger or more patient; I feel like a seventh grader again ... unsure of myself. This new relationship—where is it going? Do I even want it to happen? I want to see the future so I know if this guy is worth investing my time in.

I'm not playing games with Mr. H. I just decided I'm not going to be led by my emotions for once. I'm not going to expect a profession of undying love in the first two weeks. My past relationships have been—shall we say—dramatic, intense, and fast. I thought it was due to my being a hopeless romantic. Now I see it was because I was hopelessly impatient and wanted to cut to the chase every time. I chose men that were more than willing to go there with me.

Rushing into things goes against my southern upbringing. The whole old-fashioned way of dating is very southern. The man courts the woman, which is great if the woman doesn't pull her hair out wondering what the man's intentions are. I've never mastered the whole demure, southern belle thing. I don't like waiting for any-thing—a phone call or an email. It makes me feel vulnerable. I hate that. I mean, who wants to feel vulnerable in any way? That might involve rejection and I think we'd all agree—if we could avoid rejec-tion for the rest of our lives, we would.

I know this dating process is supposed to be fun and easy, but it's sort of annoying. I hate not knowing where it's going. It's too early to know if this is a guy I'd have a potential relationship with, but I still want to know. I don't want to waste one second of our time if it's not in God's will. I've always said I believe there should be a card system or some kind of signal to deal with relationship rejec-tion—especially at the beginning, when someone you don't want to date expresses interest in you and they just don't get the hint. We could have a green card for "Yes, I like you. Please proceed" and a red card for "I don't think so; this means *stop* calling!" Wouldn't that be simple, clean, and nice?

I see now I've built up some bad habits from my past relation-ships that are hard to break: Right from the start Mr. H. and I spent all our time together so we were completely attached and subjective. We didn't allow anything to grow naturally; we just jumped on the emotional roller coaster and stayed there. The highs were exhilarat-ingly high and the lows made me want to throw up!

With this new situation I'm taking things relatively slow. I've seen Mr. H. about once a week for three weeks. Our dates have been traditional and don't go until the wee hours of the morning. I haven't jumped in with both feet. I've kept my heart in a guarded place with lots of prayer. I like him and he makes me laugh. We've seen movies and gone out to dinner with friends, and nothing out of the ordinary has happened, except the more I spend time with him the more I like him. I even sat through *Planet of the Apes* for him!

He calls consistently. He hasn't missed a beat. Any issues that have come up have existed solely in my head. It's like I'm looking for him to make a mistake so I can bolt out the door. I'm very protective because I don't want to go through this process again and get hurt. But I have to go through it, don't I? Don't we all? Yes—unless we go back to arranged marriages. And that's an idea I've strongly considered at times. (Just kidding!)

We also have to face up to the fact we all have these tapes playing in our heads, "What if this doesn't work out? What if we aren't compatible? What if I hurt his feelings and lead him on? Or vice versa?" This kind of thinking should not be occupying a lot of time in our heads. I think the only weapon for me here to fight my female anxiety is prayer. We have to keep putting our trust in God. I personally have to do this on a continual basis. I remember that he has the perfect partner picked out just for me, whom he will reveal in his time. But when, God? When? Is this him? Does this feel right? What is right anyway? If it was right, wouldn't I know?

You can't blame a girl for asking!

46

tennis match

Why does dating seem like a tennis match to me? It's like each person is trying to score points and gain control:

Don't call + 1 point

Call −1 point

Return call + 0 points

It's like you want to seem interested but not too interested — available but independent. I know this is not God's design for how it all should go, but our own human conception makes it more complicated than ever.

Oh, Lord, help me. I'm a weak woman. I talk a big game, but put me on the court and I drop the ball — several times. It's so easy to embrace the concept of waiting on God when you're alone — you don't think you have a choice. But when a man enters the picture and starts pursuing you, you still have to wait on God — more than ever! I've never done it, but I'm attempting to wait on God in my current situation.

Mr. H. is the kind of guy who makes my knees weak when he walks into a room. I'm reduced to nervous laughter and unable to form complete sentences! I just keep praying, but I feel so weak sometimes and temptation is so strong in all areas. Just because we try to commit to having a pure relationship and godly boundaries doesn't mean it's going to be easy. I'm actually afraid I won't be able to do it 100 percent. I can rationalize almost any behavior; I've been doing just that my whole life. Trying to stick to God's guidelines is more than difficult right now, and I doubt it will get easier.

I'm learning to "crucify my flesh" ... in other words, to do the opposite of what I'd normally want to do. For example, if I truly want to be pursued and courted in the traditional way, I have to give up my control to some degree. I can't be picking up the phone whenever I feel like talking to him. Not that calling a guy is a bad thing, but I want to leave him room to be the pursuer, right? Where are the guidelines? Where's the book of biblical dating? Why did the apostle Paul leave that letter out?

I think there are a lot of passive men out there, and a lot of women like myself who will just take the reins in the beginning of a relationship and control it the whole time. I have a strong personality and that's what comes naturally to me, but I know that is not what God wants for me ... and that is not what I truly want for myself. So I have to look at every relationship, no matter how new or casual, as setting the foundation for something more serious down the line. Why wait and then try to fix it later? First of all, that almost never works. Jake, my ex of two years, and I tried that when we both started realizing how God wanted things to be, but it didn't work. After doing it our way for a year, we tried to start over and date "God's way." It was so difficult. We were already set in our roles and had crossed a lot of boundaries; it was almost impossible to go back. Once we cleared all the junk out we saw that we just weren't a match.

With Mr. H. I'm trying my best to learn patience and really surrender this whole process to God. I'm waiting to see if it's God's will for me to be spending time with this man. I'm really up in the air right now. I don't have complete peace either way, but it's only been a month and it's been going pretty slowly. As you know by now, I usually don't "do" slow very well, but it's going okay. We spend a lot of time talking on the phone but about half of that is spent joking around, which is fun too. So it's not like we're having these intense, soul-searching conversations.

Don't get me wrong! I love soul-searching conversations, but I'm saving them for a little bit later. Even talking intensely on the phone can be a type of emotional bonding. You share your deepest longings and secrets; it can be very intimate. I'm not doing that so soon again. A guy has to earn my trust now ... and vice versa.

I know all this sounds very prim and proper, and maybe I'll actually stick to it this time ... this courting, taking-it-slow thing. Maritza, my mentor from church, has given me some good guidelines about all this, and I think she is basically trying to help me avoid flying off to "la-la love land" in the first thirty minutes of a relationship. So I'm willing to try it her way, assuming this is also God's way. It's really going to be up to God to ultimately guide me, if I'd just slow down long enough to listen to him. I'm trying though ... I really am.

47

spiritual leader

I've told myself and Mr. H. that I want the man to be the spiritual leader in a relationship. I think this is something I really want ... not some catchphrase I've heard thrown around in church. But in all honesty I don't even know what a spiritual leader looks like in a relationship. Is it some dude who carries his Bible everywhere and prays for me all the time? Beats me! Not a lot of sermons on that topic lately!

The thing is, I have these control issues and I want to be in charge all the time. It's my nature to be dominant. I can't help it—I'm Italian! The world teaches, "I'm a strong woman of the new millennium. If I want something done I'll do it" and "I don't need a man to make me happy." That's all well and good, but it's not how I want my relationships to be. I do desire a man with a strong personality who will take charge sometimes ... I think. It's so confusing. Maybe I'm just saying that because I've heard it in church and think that's what I'm supposed to say. I wish I knew how God feels about dating relationships. I mean, they didn't pull us aside in gym class in sixth grade and separate the girls from the guys and give some lecture on how to assume the proper female role in a dating relationship! I'm really riding by the seat of my pants here. But there are a couple things I do know.

My past relationships have been wrong. I've met some married couples whom I admire, and they must have done something "right" when they dated. So I ask a lot of questions of them and try to form my own opinions from there.

I see my old habits creeping in. I'm running to lots of people for advice on the topic. I don't want to screw it up again. I don't want to be with the wrong guy for one single day. I just want the crystal ball to tell me how this is going to play out so I can know what to expect. Is that so wrong?

I know what I want in a man. I've even made my top-ten list and presented it to God. So now what? Does this mean that if a guy doesn't exhibit all of the qualities on my list, he's out? I'm not talking about the superficial stuff—I'm talking about spiritual qualities.

For example:

1. A man whose life is a reflection of his devotion to God.
2. A man who will pray with me and *for* me and encourage me in my spiritual walk.
3. A man who will put God above everything else in his life, even me.

In addition, I listed sixteen other qualities, ranging from kindness, to sense of humor, to being a good dancer. I just thought I'd put it all out there, and why not? God wants the best for me, right? When I broke up with Jake after two years, I said to myself, "The next one better be good" because Jake was a great guy; he just wasn't God's best for me. I also said that after Joshua and a couple others. This seems to be a pattern, and where will it end? I sure don't know.

48

rock the boat

I called my mentor, Maritza, who is always there with God's truth and speaks it to me boldly in love. Bold is an understatement sometimes, but I love her for it. I've been updating her on my progress. I explained to her that I just wasn't feeling good about this new dating relationship, and I felt uneasy and didn't know why.

"My dear little Juliet (she calls me), it's clear to me you're in this state because at some point you made this young man more important than God!" What? How did I do that? No way! I don't even like him all that much; not like guys in the past. And I've been so careful and prayed about this at every step! This is crazy! What guy is more important than God? But maybe she had a point; I was sick to my stomach over something.

Maritza challenged me to ask God when the moment was that Mr. H. became more important. I'd try anything to get my head on straight, so I asked God. It came to me in an instant. I didn't like the answer, but it was unmistakably from my Father God—the first time we were alone together. All I can say is, according to the world's standards, we had an innocent night watching television. But according to God's standards, I gave in to the desires of my flesh. I know that sounds so cheesy, but that is what they call it in the Bible, so that is how I'm stating it here. You know what I'm talking about.

I remember the first time he kissed me. He and I were at a party and he walked me to my car. We did our usual sarcastic banter thing and I could sense the tension was there. I finally couldn't take it anymore and started rambling about how I knew he wanted to kiss me. Before I could finish, he placed his hands on my face, leaned in slowly, and laid one on me. I felt it to the bottom of my toes. It was just like the movies ... all we needed was a rain storm and it would have been perfect. I could barely stand up and we kissed and kissed against my car until I forgot my name and it was time for me to attempt to drive home. It was amazing and passionate and I forgot the rest of the evening. All I could replay in my mind was our "long, slow goodnight." This was trouble and I knew it.

I've changed gradually and am so different about this physical stuff than I used to be. None of this would have bothered me before, but the next morning there was just this sinking feeling in my gut that my behavior the night before was less than exemplary. But that was the old pattern and I was just doing what came naturally. The whole "we're two consenting adults thing" kept playing in my head, and I was patting myself on the back for being so conservative compared to others, as if God grades on a sliding scale. I'm sure God's up in heaven looking down on me saying, "What? You want a cookie?"

Sound dramatic? It wasn't at the time. It's not like anything bad happened; we just cuddled and made out for awhile ... okay, three hours, but who's counting? Enough said. But where was my heart? Where was his mind? Where was *my* mind? Not where it should have been, I can tell you that! That night was one of the most passionate, lustful nights I've ever spent with someone. Yes, I behaved myself, according to the world's view. Yes, I got up and went home, actually feeling like I had been good for not letting things go too far. But now we were bonded on that physical level and that could only make me feel more vulnerable and more needy ... not good!

I thought I was fine and was fighting to stay as guarded as I could. Yes, I felt a little convicted the following day, and we even discussed it on the phone. But it was so much fun and it met my needs for that physical affection, so I continued to rationalize and just moved on. I didn't think about my behavior much after that first night.

We kept talking on the phone and seeing each other at social functions. He was a great date at parties ... friendly, flirtatious, and fun. He had this one blue sweater, that when he wore it, I was a goner. I still remember my friend Trista had a party and he walked in wearing this sweater, and I literally got goose bumps, not to mention bragging rights to all my friends about how hot my new guy was. That night he walked me to my car and we shared a long, passionate goodbye, full of lip locking.

But then I went over to his place again and it was the same story. It reminded me of high school and two crazy kids pushing the envelope without technically breaking any rules. Whose rules? I don't know, but it seemed fine. I knew it wasn't really fine, but I didn't want to rock the boat and stop anything. Maybe I was afraid he wouldn't want to be with me. This was all so new; I really felt like I was grasping for straws trying to find the guidelines here.

I guess it had been affecting my emotions about him too. Once we were physical in even the smallest way, I felt so much more vulnerable than before, and I didn't like it. It's not like God made these rules about physicality to punish me; I know it's to protect me from this exact situation. I can't go on dating Mr. H. if I wake up anxious about us all the time.

I realized later that I've never really stood up for God and his principles in any of my relationships; I'd just go with the flow and when it got to be too much to handle, God would help me find a way out and I'd vow to start over. Sometimes I would be too weak to leave a relationship, even though I knew I should because that person wasn't God's best for me. Then the guy would break up with me. Looking back, it was a blessing. I knew with Mr. H. that something had to change. But how? Was God calling me to rock the boat and say something this time? This was going to be scary.

49

girlfriends

The one difference in my relationship with Mr. H., as opposed to others, is that I had friends praying for me this time. Yes, I'm serious! I have friends that actually care enough about my well-being to pray about my dating life! It's amazing! One of God's greatest blessings to me has been my Christian girlfriends. If I started to name names, we'd be here forever, but they know who they are. They are the ones who take my neurotic phone calls, and rather than allowing me to rant and rave, they tell me they're praying for me or they pray with me right then and there. Praying is the best thing a girlfriend can do for her friends. I never thought I'd take prayer over shopping, but I have to confess that prayer is quicker therapy—and much cheaper in the long run. We also do our fair share of what my friend Trista calls "retail therapy" and what I call "chocolate therapy."

I've had many validation partners in my life. I just call them and then ramble a whole story in the hopes that they will blindly agree with me. That is *supposed* to make things better. Some of my girlfriends go back with me throughout the years and have lived through almost every single dramatic experience with me. God bless them; they know who they are. Susie Koster and I bonded in the eighth grade girls' locker room over our lack of volleyball skills. And then

Jules and I bonded on our way to music school over whatever frat boy I was flirting with the night before. But the way I relate to my girlfriends lately is different.

My girlfriends have now given me accountability. It means that if I'm not driving home at a reasonable hour, I will have some explaining to do in the morning. It's not that there would ever be judgment, but just someone to call it like it is. If I say I want to walk uprightly with the Lord and this is how I am going to do it, then I have women who will hold me to that standard. And if I fall, they will be there to pray with me and find ways to help me not let it happen again. They are not afraid to speak the truth in love. They tell me when I'm about to make a huge mistake, and that has been invaluable. I don't need sugarcoating. Jesus never did that. I need godly women who will encourage me to seek a pure and holy walk with the Lord. They are my rocks—they understand my struggles because they've been there. We have each other to get through this crazy life. For them, I am eternally grateful.

50

worth the struggle?

Things have been up and down in my little mind. Putting all this wisdom I've managed to acquire into practice is beyond difficult. As much as I complain, it's so nice and safe to be alone. No one can hurt me or disappoint me or cause me to be vulnerable. It's easier to stay on the sidelines and just watch all the other players.

In the short time Mr. H. and I have been seeing each other, I have learned so much about myself. All my insecurities did not magically disappear on my dating hiatus; they were still there. I just have to remember to submit them to God.

Part of me wanted to run away from dating him at the slightest disappointment. I was looking for reasons to bolt. I even tried to give him "my speech"—the one I had rehearsed over and over in my head about why we had to break up—but he wouldn't let me.

He actually fought for me. He encouraged me not to back away from this relationship because I was scared of being vulnerable. I knew it was something more than being vulnerable that was making me want to jump ship. I just couldn't put my finger on it. He was just so charming that I stopped wondering for a bit.

The older I get, the harder this relationship thing is. I've given my heart away too many times and each time I've been hurt. It has made me cautious—and even fearful. It used to be more casual; when one relationship ended I just looked for another. But now there is more at stake, and I'm not willing to let my heart open up so easily. I realize I've never done it God's way; he would never have wanted me to experience all that pain and heartache. But now I'm determined to have a relationship God will be proud of.

This is not easily done—not by a long shot. First of all, I'm dating a guy I'm so physically attracted to I can't even stand it. And yet, I'm supposed to keep my thoughts and actions pure. But if you ladies could see him! Can I just say he has a six pack? Yummy! I'm a weak woman, I tell you. But what is the alternative? Go out with someone I'm lukewarm about? Can't do it! So we're battling the sexual temptations and it's hard. So hard! I don't know how these other couples do it. Maybe it's because they walk around not holding hands, singing "Kumbaya" for a few months and then get engaged and married within a year. Then they're free to do whatever they please, whenever they please. Well, God bless 'em, but that hasn't happened for the rest of us.

Have we been perfect in our quest for purity? No, but God is faithful and he knows our hearts. It's funny—the world would tell me that being physically affectionate—and even intimate—is a natural and vital part of any relationship. But God tells us that stuff should be saved for marriage—even those actions that seem mild to the rest of the world.

It's amazing how quickly I'm convicted if I cross over a line. But it's annoying because a few years ago, most of this didn't bother me. I didn't think about there being lines to cross in dating; it was just meet someone and give, give, give. Give 100 percent and then if it doesn't work out, you can still say you gave it your all. Well, I've found out that is not God's design. We brilliant humans came up with that relationship model.

Since I've submitted my love life to the Lord, he has gently shown me that he wants to protect me from getting too attached to someone who is not my husband. It's not something I can put into words, but it's a real feeling in my heart. It's like I have this love that is sacred and valuable, and my innermost thoughts and feelings are meant to be shared with that one special person, not the several special people that come into my life before him. I hope one day when I meet my husband it will have been worth all this struggle. I know my past isn't perfect but I'm trying. I really am. I know this will be worth it. Right, God?

51

the talk

So I did it. Okay, we did it. Whatever. We had this long conversation as I started to launch into my breakup speech one day. I just couldn't take it anymore; I had to say something and I was so frustrated with myself. I thought breaking up would be the easiest option. I was convinced Mr. H. wouldn't want to date me if I was going to be so conservative—especially since I had been giving him mixed signals. I was still trying to figure things out too.

I rambled some more and stuttered and cried a little, but I got my point across that I didn't want to have the physical stuff crowding our objectivity. I said we shouldn't be tempting ourselves by pushing the envelope. He surprised me, because instead of rejecting the idea and pushing me out the door, he said, "Okay. You tell me where the line is and that will be that." What? I was relieved but scared at the same time. I think part of me wanted to get out of the relationship and be safe and alone again. That way I wouldn't have to deal with any of this stuff. Back to the sidelines and I'd just cool off for awhile. I was learning that the grass is always greener...

Now to be honest, I knew he didn't have the same convictions about this stuff that I did. His line was a little to the left of mine, but for my sake he was willing to do this. I'm praying God will convict his heart to be on the same page as mine because I can't carry this burden on my own. Most guys — even Christian guys — would have thought I was nuts. It's just that a lot of people have different boundaries than I do. Who's right? It's between each person and God, but the feeling in my heart when I'm going against God's will for me is so real and unmistakable I can't deny it.

52

one strike and you're out!

It's been almost three months since I've been with Mr. H., and I spent the whole first month looking for reasons *not* to date him. It's like I have this checklist for the perfect man and if he misses one bullet point he's out — or I'm out — of the relationship. Do you like how I relate relationships to sports? It shows my type-A competitive nature. Will I ever learn that dating is not a game, and there doesn't have to be a winner and a loser? I see that all this is based on my fear and my mistrust of God being in control. I'm bound and determined to do it myself — the hard way — the way that has failed every single time in my past relationships.

Mr. H. is turning out to be a pretty great and consistent guy — no games and no roller coaster. But I keep going from high to low in my little head. If we have a good date, I'm high; if I don't get a call when I expect it, I'm low. Of course, he doesn't know any of this is going on. He'll figure it out when he reads this book. Hopefully, I'll be recovered by then!

He's a good listener, and if something comes up that hurts or disappoints me, I can tell him. He takes it in and usually does something about it. For instance, once I told him I was disappointed. We had made plans for him to come see my place several times, and it hadn't worked out. (It's about a forty-minute drive for him.) He came down that evening and the next because he knew that was important to me. Nice move! Two points!

Mr. H. and I spent a couple weeks apart over Christmas, and since we've been back together he's really been winning me over on many levels. We've had some great talks, opened up to each other, and it feels safe because we're still taking things slowly. Yet there is something I don't have peace about and I can't put my finger on it. I'm usually so head-over-heels by this point and so wrapped up in roses and emotions that I can't see straight. Maybe the fact that this hasn't happened yet has me uneasy.

We've been hanging out in groups, which takes care of any physical temptation. I also feel safe because that part of the relationship isn't in play. I feel like I'm honoring God and getting to know this man on a personal level. Did I just call him a man? I usually say "boy." Guess I am growing up!

I'm trying not to sweat the small stuff and to allow God to show us both if this is a relationship he wants us to pursue. I don't want to compare it to any past relationship, my friends' relationships or marriages, or other people's expectations of what is "right" or not. I also can't compare it to the whirlwind I just went through this summer with Joshua. That was amazing but so out of control, fast, and emotional. I don't know how either of us survived it and actually managed to salvage a friendship out of it. It's got to be about God and waiting on the path he has set out for me.

53

watching a movie

Tonight we have a date to get dinner and then watch his favorite movie. It's a foreign film which I usually hate, but I'm trying to be accommodating, and I think it's romantic he wants to share this with me. My friends have already told me not to go to his apartment alone again. I know! I know! But it's so tempting, and I'm bound and determined to be an adult about this. We can't always be in groups ... and I like movies! I'm a grown woman—are these friends really convinced I can't conduct myself in a mature manner for three hours on a Friday night? Ridiculous!

Okay, it's a given that I have never made it through "watching" an entire movie with a boyfriend without some massive make-out session, but I'm going to do this even if it kills me. I keep repeating to myself "I think I can! I think I can! I think I can!"

I'd rather be frustrated and risk a guy rejecting me for standing up for what I believe in than to give in physically and have to deal with the guilt afterward. Really, all that nausea just isn't worth it! There is always victory on the other side when we stand our ground for the Lord. I think I can! It's a first for me and I'll see what happens.

Well, you're not going to believe this, but I did it! I emerged victorious! I got through a whole movie without attacking him or vice versa! This is a big deal for me. Judge me if you will, but I felt so accomplished as I drove home from Mr. H.'s place last Friday night, though again I can just see God sitting up in heaven saying, "What Kerri? Do you want a cookie?" Okay, so we barely were able to control ourselves, but we did. We really did! Victory!

There were just a couple of weak moments after the movie, in another one of our looong goodbyes that had become notorious. But overall I felt good about my accomplishment, knowing my previous track record. Once again, hoping God grades on a sliding scale. I'd give myself a B+ and two pats on the back.

And guess what? I went over there before a party the next night with my new-found confidence. We had another long discussion/ debate about physical boundaries, the definition of lust, what's right, and what's wrong. He was arguing with me on the technicalities as he always seemed to do.

I felt strong; I spoke boldly about purity, waiting on God, and saving myself for marriage on all levels. Mr. H. listened, but plainly argued he didn't exactly see it the same way I did. He said he couldn't find my rules in the Bible. So we took out the Bible that was on his coffee table and I did my best sermon. We even looked up "lust" in the dictionary and talked some more. Then he and I agreed where to draw the line—like we always did. I felt good. I felt strong!

What do you think happened next? With the Bible concordance still open on the coffee table, I gathered my purse and jacket to leave. We were going to a birthday party together that night. We gave each other a hug to celebrate our new boundaries, and then another, then a kiss and another. The boundary line so recently drawn was crossed and that was that. We never made it to the party.

I don't need to go into detail, but you know what "too far" feels like. I felt the conviction in my heart but my head has some kind of switch that allows me to turn off the Holy Spirit. That's exactly what I did. It actually worked too, for a little while. We even joked—I called it being on "planet Kerri" and said I didn't want to come back to earth because I knew it would be too painful. It was bad ... but I was in no mood at the time to try to turn back. Reality would set in and I would have to deal with it, but I was having too much fun to think about that ... at least at the time.

I think people have this view of Christians as little Bible-reading robots that do not have sexual desires—as if we really do have some "off" switch we can use before we get married and then *bling, bling*, it goes on for the honeymoon. Wouldn't that be nice? But it's not anywhere near the truth. Trust me! It doesn't matter if you're sixteen or twenty-six, the rules on purity remain the same if you're single, and it certainly doesn't get any easier as you get older. I just want to be real here because we're not perfect and sometimes we screw up.

No, a lot of times we screw up! I went around for a long time thinking that once you really dedicated your life to following Christ, you didn't make mistakes and you led this totally pure "'Kumbaya'-singing" life. Again, not true. I think it's a lie from the enemy so we keep feeling unworthy and not holy enough for God. Where in the Bible does Jesus turn away sinners? In fact, it's the opposite. He said those who have sinned much will be forgiven much. Now I'm not saying it's good to go out and rip it up and then say you're sorry. Jesus said, "If you love me, keep my commandments." The more I walk with God the more I want to do just that. And I'm trying every day. I really am! Which makes it all the harder when I fall down.

The Holy Spirit makes it easier to walk in a pure way, but we live in a fallen world and we are sinners; things don't always go the way we plan. But God is so gracious. He lets us learn from our mistakes; that way we're not inclined to make that same mistake the next time. I'm a little hardheaded, so sometimes God takes me around the same mountain several times before I get it—which is what I was learning once again in my relationship and actions with Mr. H. God's Word tells us he's there to forgive us each time and to fill us with his love and grace. That's the part that is so hard for me to grasp sometimes because I am filled with this total and utter sense of unworthiness. He gives so much and asks so little ... so why does it seem so hard?

54

reality bites

The morning after my "falling off the wagon" at Mr. H.'s house, reality set in, of course. Big time! There I was, nauseous with pain and feeling too embarrassed to pray. Even when I did pray, I didn't feel better. I was just beating myself up in true Kerri fashion from all those guilty years of Catholicism. Ironically, Mr. H. doesn't suffer from that guilt. Even though he's Catholic, he's all about God's grace. He even bought me a book, *How Good Do We Have to Be* that was written by a Jewish rabbi on the subject of guilt. In Mr. H.'s mind, I was seriously afflicted with guilt and he was not. Hmmmm, "Hello, Kerri! Get out now!"

After a couple of long talks, it occurred to me he wasn't as convicted as I was about our previous actions. I was grieved about them and he was "uncomfortable," as he put it. I just wondered why God would convict me with such a vengeance, to the point where the boundaries I must now live within seemed quite strict. I was unable to comprehend why God would not convict Mr. H. in the same manner. We both pray, we both read the same Bible. It was maddening, and I wondered how we could continue dating if we were on such different pages. He agreed to the boundaries I told him I wanted, yet we didn't follow them. I knew I needed a teammate who would be happy to help me stay 100 percent pure, not just 80 percent.

So of course, we agreed to stay out of each other's apartments. That was the only way we could guarantee that nothing like that would happen again. He came down to see me for a date and we went skating with some friends. We had the best time. It was awesome; he was a perfect gentleman. I think part of the attraction Mr. H. had for me is that my friends seemed to really like him. He was such a charmer, and I just felt good being around him. Like I said, he was great at parties!

We had a long talk that night and he explained that he took it personally when I told him how bad I felt about the previous weekend and our behavior. He thought that I meant I felt bad about being with him. This should have been another sign to me that we were in two different places. I just kept hoping and praying God would convict his heart. We seemed so close on this issue, but not totally in sync, which caused frustration on both our parts. Looking back, we weren't really close at all.

After our skating date that night, I felt lighter. I felt respected. I felt good and pure in the eyes of the Lord. This is what I wanted to be the norm. If we were to keep the physical out of it, then we could be objective about the future of our relationship—if there was to be one. I know this may seem like I was talking a lot about a future with this guy, but I didn't want to be with him one more day if it wasn't God's will. I was not about wasting anyone's time.

55

romance, romance

There were other factors missing for me at that point. As wonderful as Mr. H. was, I communicated to him on the phone one night that I wanted more of a sense of romance from him. I felt cared for, I felt like he was unbelievably attracted to me, but I wanted the girlie stuff. He was excellent at making me feel physically attractive, no question. But I wanted to know what he was feeling toward me on some other level. I guess I was searching for his intentions. I didn't know where he was coming from at all, and I was hoping he would tell me through a card, a note, a flower … I hadn't seen any of that, and I told him those types of gestures were important from both of us. My father wrote the book on that kind of love language. He was always showering mom and me with gifts and cards and affirmations of how special we were. Is it wrong to just want a guy to write me a love note one day or even buy me a silly card or token of his affection? I had these types of things before from my exes, but they weren't Christian. Now I want it all! But maybe there aren't romantic Christian guys out there. At least not funny ones I'm attracted too. Should I just settle?

Needless to say, it was hard for me not to be receiving those kinds of romantic gestures. I just wanted Mr. H. to write me a note or do something sweet. Was that too much to ask? He listened and took in everything I said; he was good at that. So at least I gave him all the information and waited to see what he would do with it. I wasn't asking for a lot of material things—just whatever "romantic" meant to him. He knew I liked flowers, so what more could I do at that point?

I spent a week after our "romance talk" and skating date praying hard every day. I tried to fast a couple mornings and that helped, I think. I prayed for God to give me a sign—a big one where he hit me over the head with a two-by-four. In my past relationships I had jumped in heart first—there wasn't a lot to ask God about. My prayers consisted of thanking God for this wonderful new man that I had handpicked; I never stopped to ask God's opinion. This time it was different. I needed peace about Mr. H. and I didn't have it ... but I wouldn't stop trying to get it either.

God revealed a lot to me that week. I read his Word every day and he showed me his abundant love. He doesn't want me to have any fear of that love wavering. No matter what I do or how many times I fall, his love is still the same and he's always there to pick me up again. Now I realize how hard that concept is to grasp; how many of us have ever experienced true unconditional love? Even love from our own families can seem to have strings attached. I realized that, while growing up, I wanted to be good and stay out of trouble so my parents wouldn't get angry. I was afraid they wouldn't feel the same way about me.

But you know, the Bible is filled with examples of God's total and unfailing love for us. Romans 8:38–39 says, "For I am convinced that neither death nor life, neither angels nor demons, neither the present nor the future, nor any powers, neither height nor depth, nor anything else in all creation, will be able to separate us from the love of God that is in Christ Jesus our Lord." That about covers everything, don't you think? That means no matter how many ridiculous mistakes we make, God still loves us!

Now what that also meant to me was that if I trusted in God's love, I'd know he wouldn't leave me hanging in a state of limbo about a relationship. So I kept praying and leaning on his promises. He promised not to give up on me. He always hears my cries. And I cried to him for help—every day and every night—"Lord, help me to hear your voice. Give me a spirit of power and a sound mind. Lord, give me direction. Don't let me stay in this relationship one more day if it's not your will." I laid my requests before the Lord and again wrote down my list of qualities I desired in a godly partner.

As the days passed I felt stronger, more at peace, closer to hearing God's voice. I felt refreshed and totally forgiven for anything and everything in my past. I realized that when I sinned I didn't need to beat myself up emotionally. I needed to get on my knees, repent, and cry out to God. I also saw that God loves me enough to make my heart sensitive to my own rebellion. It would be a scary place if I could go on in rebellion and not even notice it. I've been in that place before, and I don't want to go back there.

I'm thankful that the Holy Spirit won't let me stray too far these days. It may seem crazy to others when they see how my life has changed. My choices have become radically more conservative, but I don't care what others think. I know I'm right where God has placed me and there is victory in that ... and peace.

Mr. H. and I made plans to go to dinner. I hadn't seen him for a week and I was excited. I had spent this past week in a lot of prayer about this relationship. I think in my gut I knew what I was supposed to do, but I kept telling God I needed a clear sign. The minute we saw each other I felt that unmistakable chemistry between us. The feelings were strong and I got goose bumps. We chatted at his apartment just for a bit before we left. He looked so good ... he smelled so good. He was so complimentary of my attire that evening. We managed to actually leave the apartment, but not before an hour or so of innocent affirmations of how much we missed each other. I think my blood pressure rose about a hundred points.

We had a lovely dinner out that night. Afterward we walked and talked throughout the city streets holding hands. At one point he pulled me close, right there on the crowded street, and kissed me. This, of course, made my knees weak. I loved the fact that he didn't care who was around and that he was so affectionate.

As I was engrossed in my "movie moment," a lady selling roses approached us. Immediately he waved her off with a "No, thank you." My heart sank. The music in my head stopped playing. Yes, I was hurt! Why? Because in three months I had never received a single flower from him, or anything of the sort, even though I had told him I desired that kind of stuff. We even specifically talked about flowers once ... he knew these things were really important to me.

All I could think of at that moment was "Wow! You like me enough to make out with me in the streets but not enough to buy me a stupid flower!" You might call me high-maintenance, but I don't think I am. I think it was a clear sign from God—"Kerri, he's not that guy who will buy you flowers or send cards, write poems, or do the romantic things you want! Accept the facts." I didn't say anything and we went on with our date. I just looked at him and once again was lost in his appearance; my emotions took off as he reached for my hand.

He drove me back to his place where my car was and we started to say our goodnights. Usually this could take anywhere from one to three hours. Not kidding! Our first kiss lasted two hours and we've pretty much used that as the standard ever since.

Now I need to address something here. I know there will be certain people reading this, especially from my church, who don't believe I should have been kissing Mr. H. at all. Radical? I know! I still can't picture myself in a relationship without any physical affection, but a lot of people have felt convicted to date this way and ended up in great marriages. All I can say is that the more we pray specifically for God to reveal his truth, the more he will. We will find our own boundaries and feel a sense of peace about them. If you had told me three, or even two, years ago that I would be so far over to the right on this issue, I wouldn't have believed you. But it happened.

Anyway, back to the date. We're in the car, which is a safe place, right? I mean, we're not in high school — what can happen in a car? Ha! With this guy, things could get heated up in a freezer! He gets within three feet of me and it's over. Except for the fact that my dad was not coming out of the house onto my driveway with a gun, it was the eleventh grade all over again.

It only took a few minutes for me to see where the situation was going and to bring it to an abrupt and unexpected stop. Things had already gone too far in my opinion, but I didn't back off right away. This was par for the course with us. I'd say one thing, then do another and lose all credibility with him. And he didn't feel convicted that any of this was wrong, so he didn't feel he should stop. According to his outlook, we were being way good comparatively. It was only natural that a little bit of this would happen because we were so into each other. I didn't agree and he knew it. This discussion had taken place so many times, it was like clockwork whenever we saw each other. I'd tell him how I felt, he'd tell me his view, and I'd go home hoping things would change the next time. I'd always wake up nauseous the next morning.

So guess what? As usual, we started the same discussion, but this time we were both upset. I was upset because I wanted a team player — someone who would hear my boundaries, respect them, and then help me stick to them. Was it too much to ask to find a man who actually had some boundaries like mine? He said we were grown adults and we should be able to do what we wanted to, within reason. This was maddening. I had said it backwards, forwards, and in every language I knew; for whatever reason it wasn't getting through!

I was totally weak when I was around him — even though he wouldn't call it weak, but being human — and he didn't do anything to help matters. I realize he wasn't convicted like I was; it must have sounded radically conservative to him. But even so, if he cared about my happiness and peace of mind, why couldn't he have helped keep things cool when that's what I kept saying I wanted? He didn't view it as not respecting me—he saw it as two healthy adults who were in a serious relationship exercising a lot of restraint. If we were 80 percent there, then what's a little gray area? Did he not care that this type of behavior practically brought me to tears every time?

Everything he said that night I had heard before, but it was finally sinking in. I was just waiting for that final blow so I could know for sure I had to leave him. And then it came. He said, "So let me get this straight. You want a guy who is wildly attracted to you and wants to rip all your clothes off but won't come near you because you want to wait?" "Yes!" I said. "Well, good luck finding it," he said. "My church is filled with it," I answered back. "Then maybe you need to meet someone at your church!" "Fine!" I said as I headed for my car and he handed me my leftover veal marsala from our romantic dinner.

I had my sign; I just needed to get in my car and drive home. It was over and I told him so. He wanted to hug me goodbye. I couldn't even look at him, much less touch him. "Look, I can't hug you! This isn't a happy moment. I don't want to be reminded of how it feels to be in your arms or how special I feel when I'm with you. I need to go home and get over you, okay?" Tears welled up in my eyes. "Will you at least call me when you get home so I know you're safe?" "No!" I said. "One ring?" he asked. "Goodbye. Don't you realize how sad this is? We're breaking up over this! Aren't you sad?" "Of course," he said as he approached me. But what he wasn't saying was that he'd be willing to change or seek any kind of counsel from mature Christians in our lives to help us with accountability. I don't think he even knew what real accountability was!

It was obvious we could not do this on our own. He didn't want to pray with me or do anything about the situation. I had to go. I finally drove away at 3:45 a.m. My stomach was in knots. I couldn't think. I couldn't cry. My heart hurt. I had to drive. I needed to talk to someone … but not to God. He seemed a million miles away. I couldn't even begin to pray. I knew I would lose it. I decided to call Joshua, my Jewish love from New York City. It was almost seven in the morning there. He answered and I started telling him everything. He knew all about the situation. He was doing his best to form sentences since I had woken him from a sound sleep, but he was great. Even though I don't remember what he said to me, I felt comforted.

The only prayer I said on the way home was to command the excruciating cramps in my stomach to go away in the name of Jesus. I was so afraid I wouldn't be able to drive, but I made it home. Out of courtesy and selfishness, because I wanted to hear his voice, I called Mr. H. to let him know I was okay. We spoke briefly and quietly. He said, "I care about you." I said, "Not enough." "Don't say that. So I guess I won't call you tomorrow," he quickly responded. "Not unless you have something radically different to say to me—like you would be willing to get counsel from mature Christians from one of our churches." He didn't think that would be necessary, so we hung up.

How could I not have seen that we were so different? Was I that blinded by physical attraction and passion? What was that anyway? I mean, we had a great few months together but there wasn't one day I felt total peace about being with him; I just wouldn't listen to that inner voice. I thought things could change and we could work through these problems together.

As I sat in my bed that night at four thirty, I looked over at my Bible and decided to open it randomly; I was finally ready to hear from God. I opened to Song of Songs, chapter 1—a love sonnet. I knew it was from God to me. And what verse jumped out at me as my own personal love message? "How beautiful you are, my darling! Oh, how beautiful!" (Song of Songs 1:15). It was almost as if I could hear my loving Father speaking those words directly to me. I lost it! The God of the universe was telling me how much he loved me. I felt it, I knew it, and somehow I fell asleep. He had felt my pain that night. He was proud of me and was going to get me through this.

The next morning I awoke early—only three hours after going to bed—and couldn't go back to sleep. It was Sunday and I couldn't call anyone and wake them up. I decided to check my email. Out of the blue was a message from Rich, my Canadian email affair. He hadn't written me in months! He wrote, "Maybe this will be as timely for you as it is for me: 'Yet the LORD longs to be gracious to you; he rises to show you compassion. For the LORD is a God of justice. Blessed are all who wait for him!' (Isaiah 30:18)."

Rich also wrote a sweet message about waiting on God's plans for our lives and ended it with the following: "He is never ahead of schedule, never late, but always on time. Remember, if he waits longer than you wish, it is only to make the blessing more abundant when it comes." I think I'll take him up on that offer.

56

is there life after mr. h.?

Getting over Mr. H. wasn't that easy, to be honest. God didn't let me slide right into another relationship like I have done in the past—every single other time—let the record show. Even with sweet Joshua, I was dating a month after we broke up. It was seven whole months before anyone came into the picture after Mr. H., but he had no problem moving on. He began dating a girl I knew, no less. You want to talk about an ego trip? I was horrified to say the least. I should have listened to my gut way before our relationship even started!

I was good about sticking to my guns after we broke up. I'm usually good like that … once it's over, it's over. He made some half-hearted attempts at communication. He left a note on my car once … nothing romantic, just an "I miss you." I didn't call him. I drove home that night and wanted to, but I didn't call him.

He didn't call me either, and in no time at all he was dating this girl I know. I heard it third-hand too. She even knew both of us while we were dating. I didn't know who to be mad at. After I broke things off with him—well, at least I felt like I initiated it—I actually had to see them together. It was maddening. Not like I wanted him back, but I had never had this happen to me before. I didn't even know how to handle it. Mr. H. was supposed to go on the list of men that would never officially get over me ... or at least give me the courtesy of acting that way in front of my face, right? I mean, even the ones with girlfriends are still sweet to me when we talk. I know I'm over my validation issues, but nobody wants to hear from their ex all about their new girlfriend and how much better she is than you, right?

So I would hear stories about them from other people and immediately my imagination kicked in. He had turned into Prince Charming with her and decided to become the perfect flower-giving, boundary-respecting Mr. Christian. They were happily having their intention-filled, godly relationship that would someday lead to marriage. I would be forced to attend the wedding, sitting in the back row dressed in black, chain smoking, and with my gay friend like Rupert Everett in some Julia Roberts movie.

Some time went by and I prayed to God to forgive me for my lust issues with this guy, and for once again doing it my way. He forgave me the first time, but every time I felt like I wasn't over Mr. H., I would go and repent again for my behavior, asking God to completely cleanse my mind of this past relationship.

This time I wasn't really trying to find someone. I wasn't jumping online or anything like that. I was doing the things I loved and actually having a pretty great time with the important people in my life. I went to parties, traveled to different places, spent time in the Word with God, and one day I woke up and realized six months had gone by. Just like that it had been six months and I was totally single ... no crushes ... no infatuations ... no casual dating ... nothing. I had gone on hiatus and hadn't really noticed. I laughed out loud. God saw what was happening the whole time but didn't tell me because he didn't want to ruin what was going on. I was growing closer to him and learning he was the most consistent love I had ever had. I hadn't cried over anyone; I wasn't in some state of unrest. I was actually okay—more than okay. I was peaceful, happy, and I felt good. Really good.

It was weird. I had this great friendship with Josh and all these other men, but none of them were romantic and my life felt so full. How did that happen? I didn't have this sinking feeling that I would never meet someone. It was more like the feeling that I was better prepared than ever to meet the "right" someone God had for me. But who was he? Where was he? I prayed for my husband. I prayed for God to bless him wherever he was at that moment. I still haven't found him. I wonder if he's reading this book. I wonder if he's funny or neat or a good dancer. I know he's out there somewhere. I just know it.

57

what if ...

As I sit here on a Sunday night after coming home from my church picnic, I'm wondering when will it be my turn to be one of the happy couples sharing the picnic basket, sitting on the blanket together, watching our kids playing tug of war. I start thinking, *What if ... ?* What if it never becomes my turn? My love life, up until now, has been a series of great beginnings—beginnings with emotions and feeling and flowers and poetry, with all the drama of great Hollywood movies—only to leave me exactly where I am right now ... alone on a Sunday night wondering *What if...?*

I know I'm the poster child for a positive attitude on this subject; my friends depend on me to make jokes about it and to give them encouraging words like: "Yes! One day your prince will come ... and if he's with my prince, tell him to call me!"

I tell my two best friends that I'm sure our husbands-to-be are praying for us right now ... on their yacht somewhere. But what if they never make it to shore? What if I have missed him? What if my expectations and desires don't match what God wants for me, and I can't pull it together to make it work? Is that my responsibility? I know a lot of people who did *not* have their stuff together, got married anyway, and made it work. What about me? Do I have to be so perfect, so ready, so pruned, before I meet someone right for me?

Lately, I just can't figure out where God stands in my love life. I have been on a dating hiatus for a long time. I had come to a place where I was so busy with my performing, my crazy girlfriends, and my life, and I was content. I even stopped bugging God about my future husband. Can you believe it? Yes, I wanted to date, but only when the guy was someone God had chosen for me. I had said that before, and then I met Joshua and Mr. H. I don't feel that either of them was God's choice for my partner in life. So the only way for me to really ensure that the next guy would be God's choice was to take myself out of the game and go back to the sidelines for awhile, which is what I did.

I've screwed it up so many times that I just don't feel like I should take the chances any longer. I thought this was the right approach, but maybe not. What *is* the right approach to all of this? Why isn't there more about dating in the Bible? I'm just confused. I know old habits are hard to break, and in a lot of ways I'm still holding on to the fantasy: God will send my true love down from heaven, riding on a cloud, shining like the sun with a sword in his hand and a message directly from my Father God—"Yes, Kerri! This is my choice for you ... go ahead this time!"

You know, I thought about calling my dad in Georgia and asking him to arrange a marriage. My mother would have a field day with that. I'd end up married to the golf pro at the country club ... or better yet, the next plastic surgeon they ran into. My mom's new thing is that she wants me to marry a plastic surgeon so she can get a face-lift before the wedding ... for the pictures. She says she's kidding, but is she?

I guess I'm having a moment of weakness and doubt. I don't want to doubt what or who God has for me. I don't want to let the enemy come into my mind and tell me it's never going to happen, and that if it does I'll find a way to screw it up. I just think it's okay to be honest with ourselves and, more important, with God when we feel this way. I'm not writing this book to give you the magic recipe to finding true love; if I had that, I think I'd be on *Oprah* by now.

I know one thing: Through all my frustrations and even my anger, God has been there the whole time. I just wish I could have some more tangible conversations with him about this topic. If he could even give me a guarantee that I would meet my "perfect someone," I'd be happy to wait. It's just wondering *What if . . .* that kills me. Does this force me to have more faith? Does this bring me closer to God? I suppose so, but it's definitely not easy. Sometimes the "what if's" really suck.

I think I'm going to stop writing and actually talk to God about this now. That's a big step for me . . . I used to call my twenty closest friends and counselors first. Not tonight. Not this time.

58

a really hard, horrible, rotten, lonely, bad day

Dear God,

I'm lonely. As if you didn't know, I had a horrible, rotten, very bad day, and it didn't get any better as it went along. I tried to email friends, talk on the phone, mope around. I even bought myself some flowers. (What a surprise! I really shouldn't have!) Nothing worked. I talked about you and wrote emails to request lots of prayer from many people, but I didn't talk to you much. You just seemed so far away.

I'm angry about my circumstances. Why do people have to get sick and suffer? Why does cancer exist? Can't we all just drift away to heaven in our sleep?

My grandpa Eli is one of the loves of my life, and he is dying of cancer. He's so strong; he puts up a good front for me on the phone. I almost believe he's perfectly healthy ... except when I hear he's lost fifty pounds and isn't eating much at all. He laughs with me, jokes with me, tells stories about the "old days" when he met my grandmother on the dance floor during the big band era. He makes those times seem simpler—purer in some way, but I'm sure it was hard. He lived and worked through the depression. He made fifteen dollars a week working at a cigar factory, went home, and turned it all over to his mother. She then gave him a big kiss, he tells me. He had many jobs and worked for one company as a machinist for twenty-three years, only missing two days of work ... and those were Saturdays.

When I tell him I'm still not married, he laughs and says, "You know, I didn't think you'd have such a problem, honey." When I ask him how he feels he says, "I think I'll live another day." He's been saying that for twenty years now, and he's almost ninety-one. You'd think that would make it easier to say goodbye, wouldn't you? People tell me he has lived a long, full life and we should be grateful for all the time we've had with him. Well, I just say that was more time to get to know him and to love him.

He has become a love of my life; not a boyfriend or suitor that came and went, but a constant source of joy, laughter, and love. He's a positive spirit to the end. He's taught me how to take joy in simple things. Every year he fills a jar with coins and gives it to my brother and me for Christmas. He delights in seeing our eyes light up at all the silver coins as we count them on the floor. I will never outgrow this tradition. Hey, it's laundry money and I'm takin' it! He's led a simple life but it's been a good one. I've learned so much from him, and I believe I have some of his spirit ... with the exception of the not-missing-work thing. We know at this point that my career goal is trophy wife, right?

He's a fighter, and now it's my turn. God, I'm fighting for him. I don't want him to go. More important, I don't want him to suffer or lose his dignity. He's almost ninety-one and has more hair on his head than both his sons combined, and he's "strong like a bull," he tells me. He beat cancer once; why is it beyond you to help him beat it again? Why do I feel so helpless?

I don't know how to deal with this type of pain, God. I tried to escape it by running off to watch some chick flick about a woman who gets dumped, runs off to Italy, buys a house, and falls in love. I just wanted to cry, "God, why can't that be me?" I'm thinking I need some man in my life to turn to in times like this. I'm in the theater sitting next to my sweet married friends who are holding hands, and all I can do is gorge on my smuggled popcorn and hotdog! I know you were there with me, yet besides the screaming I did in my car on my way to the movie theater, there wasn't much prayer going on today. I don't know why. I don't have any answers.

You know my heart. You know I want to trust you to justify what's going on, but it's really hard right now. I want someone tangible to talk to, to get that last hug from at the end of the day, to go through these hard times with. I can't help it; that's how I feel. You say you want me to be honest with you, God, to pour my heart out to you— so here I am ... what's next? Am I supposed to go pick up my Bible and try to find comfort? I guess I could do that. I'll flip the pages until I find some verse I feel is just for me, but what if it's just me making it up?

What do you really want to say to me? Can't I just have five minutes of your time where I can really hear your voice? I know ... I know ... it's a lot to ask, but I thought I'd give it a shot. I love you always; you know that. I trust you always. You are good.

Love, Kerri

59

my best friend's wedding

Here I am, getting on a plane to attend the wedding of my best friend from college. She is marrying a prince of a man and I'm truly happy for her, and I'm not just saying that in a fake "I'm happy for her but secretly jealous" way; I really am happy. He is everything I could want for her.

Since I'm not dating anyone, I called in my Jewish love, Joshua, to be my date. After the last wedding I attended alone, I vowed not to do that again. I just enjoy slow dancing too much! It's been one year since Josh and I met in New York City. I haven't seen him since he came to California, but we've managed to form a pretty great friendship over the phone. We've talked a lot and have been there for each other through many ups and downs, joys and trials. I didn't think we'd end up being such good friends without keeping the romantic part alive, but we have and I'm so grateful.

I feel like I have been released from my romantic feelings for Joshua and I only view him as a friend, but this weekend I have to actually see him … dance with him … sit with him. I just pray God will help me hold it together. I'm not too worried. I feel like this past year I've grown so much. I've made God my rock more than ever.

I know he has my love life under control, and I am truly finished messing with it.

Josh is going to meet my parents this weekend. He said he was going to shine his shoes extra hard in order to win them over. I said, "Honey, unless you are carrying a Bible and singing 'Jesus Loves Me,' you don't have to worry about wooing anyone, myself included!" I still joke with him and tell him he should convert and marry me and we could enjoy church picnics together, much to the utter dismay of his entire family!

As much as I adore Josh, and as much as he exhibits all the amazing qualities I'm looking for — he is kind, ambitious, thoughtful; he is a wonderful friend, chef, dancer — he doesn't share my greatest passion ... the Lord Jesus Christ. And I am unwilling to compromise in my desire to share that passion and to build my marriage on it. Josh knows it too. He knows that I need to marry a man who is just as passionate about serving the Lord as I am, so he told me he wouldn't try to make things any more difficult for me. Besides, he also knows that last time when I got too attached to him, I said we couldn't talk on the phone for months. He doesn't want that to happen again. He needs my jokes too much.

Anyway, I don't think there will be a problem at the wedding; we're staying in separate hotel rooms. I'm sure my friends think that's weird, but I don't care. It's the way things have to be, and I'm fine with it.

So I guess we'll see what happens. Maybe if I sprinkle Josh with holy water at the church or look really good in my bridesmaid dress, he'll come over to "my team." He said he will be crying at the wedding when he sees me walking down the aisle ... and he doesn't even know the bride and groom. I said, "Sweetie, there's always room for one more ceremony, so if you change your mind about the Jesus thing, you just give me a sign and I'll meet ya up there!"

60

victorious

So I did it ... I emerged 100 percent victorious in what I set out to do. I saw Joshua and we spent a wonderful weekend together with friends and my family. There were no romantic entanglements to make me feel anything but absolutely thrilled to have his friendship. This is a huge milestone for me. I didn't give in to my temptations to make it some bittersweet reunion. Two lovers meet again, then go home to their respective lives like *Same Time Next Year* with Alan Alda. For those of you my age or younger who might not have heard of this movie, rent it! It's good.

Julie's wedding was wonderful. I gave a toast at the rehearsal dinner, and rather than tell jokes, I ended up getting kind of emotional and choked up; I barely held off the tears. To see the way they love each other and the way he cherishes her makes me so unbelievably happy. And the fact that Julie's husband and I bonded—let's just say he knew I came with the package when he married her. He's a good egg.

Joshua showed up at the wedding ... his first "Gentile" ceremony, and he looked as handsome as ever. I had dyed my hair a new shade of red because I wanted to be that "sassy LA girl" my friends expect me to be. Also, I'd be seeing my mother later that weekend, and I wanted to see the look on her face. Little things like that make life fun for me. Joshua complimented me immediately. He has a way of speaking that is so sincere; he always makes me feel beautiful from the inside out. The minute I saw him it was like no time had passed. We had a warm embrace and couldn't contain our smiles. Josh wanted everyone to take pictures of us every chance he got. It was cute.

Josh and I danced the night away as best we could—considering that we don't know how to swing dance. We gave it our best shot. But when they played the early 90s hip-hop, Joshua broke all the stereotypes that white Jewish men don't have moves! It was awesome. I was so glad to have him there. We slow danced and it was different than I had imagined. It was affectionate but not emotionally dramatic. I was just glad to be in his company. I did have to excuse myself to run into the ladies room for a quick prayer though: "God, he is so great, so if it's not Josh, I'm hoping you have somebody *really* good for me." That pretty much sums up my feelings for the whole weekend.

Josh became more endearing to me as the days went on. He was my cheerleader before I did a comedy show in my college town. We might as well have gotten married, because my whole extended family was there in the audience to root for me. It was like my own wedding reception without the gifts! Josh even prayed for me before the show. I told him, "If you converted right now that would really get this routine off to a great start." He is the inspiration for a lot of my act where I talk about my affections for Jewish men. I said, "I sent my ex-boyfriend a Bible and he said he only paid for part one. I told him, 'Honey, it's like *The Godfather, Part II*—ya gotta keep reading; it only gets better.'"

The long weekend ended with Josh and me spending time with my parents in my hometown. I could tell that my parents liked him, but they were perfectly clear on the situation that Josh and I were just friends. I did have my moments thinking how happy we'd make each other as partners because of all his wonderful qualities, most of all his kind and soft temperament. He'd be good for someone hot-blooded and Italian like me. I had my moments of wanting to kiss him and express romantic feelings, but they passed when I thought of the consequences. I guess I really did learn something from my past actions ... for a change, huh? Josh didn't push the issue, of course, except to tell me he was still head-over-heels for me and he'd do anything for just one kiss. He meant it, but didn't try anything because he knew that was not on the agenda.

The best part about the whole weekend was learning that in the past year Josh had really opened up spiritually to the Lord. He brought his Torah, which is the Jewish Bible—or the first five books of the Old Testament—and his yarmulke to wear on his head when he read it. We had many great discussions about God and Jesus. He had a lot of questions—so many that I became frustrated when I didn't feel equipped to answer them correctly. I just prayed and relied on the Holy Spirit to give me the words to speak to him. I have watched the Lord work in Josh's life this past year, and I pray that God's grace and love will continue to speak to his heart. I've given up praying to convert him directly so we can get married—even though I'm not opposed to the idea. I know God has a plan, and if Joshua isn't included in the plan he has for me, it's going to be somebody else *really* amazing.

The last day at the airport I got very sad having to say goodbye. I wanted Josh in my daily life. I wanted us to live closer, cook meals together, read books, and learn new things. He is the kind of friend that has so much to share. He has done so much and traveled so many places. He just returned from Israel where he swam in the same sea where Jesus walked on the water. He related to me his theory about how he thinks that actually happened. It was pretty funny.

The weekend had been filled with his kindnesses to me ... not to receive anything in return but because that is his nature. He paid for all my meals, put gas in the rental car, bought me a book to read that he thought had "Christian values"; he bought me Ben and Jerry's and gave me the last bite. He treated me the way I want to be treated by a man. If only he shared my faith—my biggest passion. He's searching, but he's not there, not really even close to seeing what I see. He doesn't experience God the way I do … his love … his grace … his personal relationship with me.

Josh is reading the Old Testament, which is filled with a lot of rules and legalism—he hasn't really discovered God's grace yet. I think the Jewish religion, as well as other religions, can get caught up in being faithful to God by following rules and living a certain standard of lifestyle, right down to the food eaten. I tried to explain to him that is not what God is about, but Josh insists that is what Moses taught the Israelites and that is how we should live now. I just hope he keeps reading and sees the difference in things when Jesus finally came. I can't believe there is a religion out there that only knows half of God's truth. They completely stop reading halfway through the Bible. Can you imagine going to a movie and leaving in the middle and just having to figure things out from there? How confusing and frustrating!

So we're sitting at the airport and Joshua decides to launch into the top fifty reasons he thinks I'm amazing. I had to stop him at fifteen. I couldn't take it anymore—had he gotten to twenty we'd have eloped to Vegas. It was his adorable way of affirming what a wonderful person he thought I was, from every angle … except one. With everything he mentioned he forgot the one thing that makes me who I am … my love for the Lord and his Son, Jesus Christ. Right then I was reminded Josh was not the guy for me. I need a man to love me and respect me, but most important, to understand that who I am today is based on my relationship with God and my desire to be more like him. Josh missed it. He had no idea, of course, and I didn't say anything, but that was my sign to hold on to as I sadly said my goodbye to him. I'm holding on to the fact that someday a man will say to me, "Kerri, the most attractive thing about you is your love and devotion to Jesus Christ and that is why I'm in love with you."

Now who will the lucky winner be? I know there has to be a Christian guy out there struggling to find some mixed-up, crazy, Italian Christian girl who's going to love and cherish him as well. Now where, oh where, could he be?

61

sunday

Dear God,

I'm up—I'm supposed to be getting ready for church. Why am I not excited? I'm wearing the pajamas an ex-boyfriend gave me. I pulled them out of the cedar chest last night and decided to write him an email just to say hi. Why? Because I was lonely ... not for him ... for just ... someone; someone to be there with me coming home on a late Saturday night and someone to get up with me Sunday morning, make me some tea, and go to church. I'm sick of going alone, facing all the people, sitting with my single friends and staring at the swarms of happy couples. I just don't think I can do it today. Is that so wrong?

I want to sit home in my flannel cloud pajamas, drink my self-made tea and sulk, pray, and then sulk some more. Is that okay? Am I hiding? Am I ignoring you, God? What do you want me to do? Go out and worship with the body of Christ? What if I just can't do it today—won't do it? I hear you say, "Okay." Is this some spiritual ploy by the enemy to keep me out of fellowship, to keep me from hearing your Word and worshiping you? Or is this just me acting like a child?

I don't have the mental resources this morning to figure it out.

My head is spinning. I spent time praying and reading this morning, confessing my selfishness to you. I asked you to make me pure hearted again ... pure minded, to take away the little bits of self-pity that have managed to creep into my heart lately. I know this is no way to be, but you said to always be honest. So here I am again; what are we going to do this time?

My life is a good one ... a blessed one. I'm realizing there is more to it than my career pursuits; I've been so focused on them these past few months. I had forgotten that you want me for me and not what I can do for you. You just want my heart, God. And I want to give it to you. I feel like sometimes I snatch it back by pursuing my own desires in my own controlling fashion.

I tried the waiting thing ... the patience thing. I put on a good face for awhile and even started to get comfortable. Then time goes by and my type-A personality impatiently rears its ugly head, wanting to be proactive. I do something like sign on to another Christian dating site, thinking I'm just "putting myself out there." The only thing that happens is I get all these emails that don't impress me.

This seems to be a birthday tradition. I have a birthday, feel older, and get antsy that I'm still alone. It's something others also seem to notice at that time. As if this is their excuse to say, "What a shame— another year has gone by and you have no one to share your life with! Praying for you!" (In that totally "I'm married," sing-songy voice).

On my last birthday I had an 80s party and danced the night away. And then in the morning, when I had finished opening my presents, I realized I was still alone. I also realized the highlight of the evening was slow dancing to REO Speedwagon with some kid in white tennis shorts who said, "Guys don't like church because they don't like being told what to do!" Happy birthday to me! Online we go!

With each year I've grown closer to you, God. I'm not as needy as the last time, but we're needy creatures; that's how you created us. I know you want us to long for you more than anything or anyone, and right now I do long for you. I need your comfort, Lord, your peace, your grace, so I can understand the situation I am in. The world tells me that as another year goes by, being alone is not good enough.

My mother is seriously getting sad and desperate about her single daughter. She thinks I need to do whatever it takes, within reason, to find someone. She used to find the whole online thing crazy; now she tells me it might not be so bad. Has she lost faith in me? My father says to take my time . . . join the convent first and then I'll be fine!

By the world's standards, am I too old? All the questions are clouding my mind and my judgment—Why don't you have someone? Why haven't you settled down by now? Are you okay? People don't see the hurt in my eyes as I put on a happy face and make some joke in response. In fact, I think if I did settle down, I'd have nothing to talk about in my standup routine. I have found the humor in all of this and that is what the world sees. They say, "Wow! You are so positive . . . you are so strong!"

But you see my heart, Lord. You see the scared little girl who just doesn't want to be alone. She never has. All along, even as a child when I feared there would be no one to play with at recess, you were there. As I felt like I would never fit in with the other kids until I proved myself and made them like me . . . you were there. You saw the hurt then and you see it now. So what am I supposed to do about it?

Where do we go from here? I'm not expecting hurts to go away once I'm married. I've been in enough relationships to know that won't happen. I've read enough books. I've seen some marriages struggle to stay alive. How much more research am I supposed to do before it's my turn? How ready and pure hearted do I have to be? Have I not submitted this process to you? Have I not waited? Have I not talked the talk and done my best to walk the walk with only a *few slipups? Am I not writing a book on the subject? I'm trying to understand your ways, God. I know your timing is perfect, but quite honestly it just seems a little slow to me.*

My thoughts turn to my sweet Joshua lately. He invited me to a family wedding in New York City this weekend. We would have danced the night away— to the dismay of his family, I'm sure. He mentioned we would take a carriage ride in Central Park. I knew I couldn't go. I didn't want his family to think that I was trying to woo their son to the "other side." I pray for him as much as I can. I pray for him to have a relationship with you, God; to see you the way I do. I want him to receive all the love and joy and grace I have because of you. When he suffers, I just pray that one of these times he'll be broken and contrite of heart enough to get on his knees and cry out to you. Maybe he has. If so, has he heard your voice? Did he recognize it? Why can't he have a conversion experience like Paul on the road to Damascus? Then he could fly to California, sweep me away, and we'd live happily ever after. I like that plan and I promise we'd use it in our testimony on our international speaking tours. What do you think, God?

Joshua has been a blessing to me and a learning tool that you have used in my life so powerfully. How did you do that? When we met, I was so self-focused and sinful, and yet you redeemed the whole situation.

One of the things Josh can't seem to understand is the conviction I feel about the way I behaved when we met. He thinks our whole relationship was so beautiful and he wouldn't want to change one single thing about it. That brings me back to square one again. No matter how caring ... how thoughtful ... how perfect I believe Joshua is, he doesn't share my convictions about life that come from my personal relationship with you. So in this moment, that leads me to believe he is not the guy ... you have someone else for me ... someone who will share those things with me and more. But how could anyone possibly be more compatible in all those other areas?

We just "fit" and yet on the most important level we don't ... not yet. Will we ever?

Do I have to completely give this up, Lord? I thought I had and the last nine months I've sat and waited ... prayed and waited on you, Lord, and asked you to bring who you have for me into my life. I've dated a couple nice guys here and there but nothing that made me really excited. Along the way Joshua and I have remained constant friends ... we've called and laughed together so many times, and when I saw him in person at Julie's wedding it was like no time had passed at all. I didn't behave badly that weekend. I followed your will for me and just enjoyed being in his company. So where does that leave me, God? Why haven't I met that person you have for me? Why do I keep thinking I already have and he's in New York City, but he just doesn't have eyes to see? I've tried my best to protect my heart.

Is today just one of those days? I'll feel blue, cry out to you, and then get up tomorrow as if nothing ever happened and go on with my single life, making other people laugh in the midst of my foibles? I feel it's deeper this time and something has to change. If I've strayed from you— even if it wasn't very far— then I want to come back. If I've watched too many chick flicks and gotten too caught up in the fantasies, then bring me back to earth. But I don't want to stop believing in the stories, God ... the hopes for a happy ending. I know you love me too much for my spirit to be broken. I won't give up my dreams, God— the dreams you gave me of a home, a family, and a partner to ride the roller coaster with. I may falter but you won't ever let me fall. I love you for that.

I thank you for listening in the midst of my loneliness. When no one else listens, you are there. I don't know the answers right now but you do. I trust that you will show them to me one moment at a time.

You are good. You are faithful.

I love you,
Kerri

62

my date with a metrosexual

Now I'm not one to consider myself too trendy, and I guess there are some things that slip by me, like the latest lingo and terms, especially ones originating from shows like *South Park*. So let me just share this little anecdote with you.

After about ten months of singlehood, I started doing the "sell-out online thing" *again* and my ego was deflated. All my friends decided to do it together so it was sort of an adventure, but not one I was taking too seriously. Now stop judging me; I know I had a stalker ... I know I haven't had any success with this online thing, but who was I to miss out on all the fun my girlfriends were having? I just thought if I could actually know that there were funny, nice, Christian guys out there, I would have renewed faith in the world of dating, so it was fine.

After awhile this nice guy and I started emailing back and forth, and soon after we decided to chat on the phone. I called him but didn't give out my number. I know it's not southern, but it's safe. We'll call him Dave. He was sweet and funny ... not hilarious, but funny enough to hold his own with me. After we spoke a couple times we made plans to meet for dinner. I had seen pictures and he was cute—almost "pretty boy" cute.

I wasn't really nervous because I knew he wasn't a serial killer. I didn't put much thought into whether it would work out or not. I was just happy to go out, have a nice dinner, and meet someone I might be attracted to.

He picked me up. I know, I know, ladies—I shouldn't have done that, but I was feeling more than comfortable after talking to him and hearing about his church and job. I'm not into cars really, but I could tell his car was fancy and it was immaculately clean. He looked good ... pretty, in a way. My first clue should have been when he wanted to discuss the wardrobe for our date on the phone before we even met. He wore a nice pair of jeans, black shoes perfectly shined, and a J. Crew button-down shirt that was white and stylish. I had on a pair of black boots that went well with my gray pants and the baby blue sweater I had purchased at Target. (I'm usually a Gap sale rack or Ross Dress for Less girl.) I had tried on several outfits because I wasn't sure what to wear, but I was happy with my choice.

I got in the car after a not-so-awkward hello and a hug. He said, "Mmm, you smell like cotton candy." I guess it was my perfume, but things were off to a good start. I was somewhat attracted to him physically, but not head-over-heels as I have been in the past with other guys. He was in great physical shape and had nice eyes and nice hair. I'd give him a solid 8.5.

We were off to have sushi and the conversation was fine; neither of us wanted to discuss how we met, that was obvious. He complimented my beach neighborhood by saying, "Well, this isn't too bad!" (As if Redondo Beach was the slums compared to his immaculate OC!)

He found it necessary to tell me his last two girlfriends were models, and that he had forgotten his diet pills at home. I have no idea what those were for, but I let it go. "Hello? Clue Phone! It's for Kerri!"

We got to the sushi place and ended up having a nice time, but I got the sense this is the kind of guy who never spills the soy sauce and if I had spilled mine, it would have been an issue. Needless to say, I spill things all the time. I get that from my mother; it's a family trait.

During dinner he did most of the talking and proceeded to work in the fact that he was homecoming king of his high school, got a scholarship to play college basketball, and spent twelve hundred dollars on sushi for his last party at his beach house, which is down the street from Dennis Rodman's. It was all very casual, and I have to give him credit for working these résumé points in; it was very smooth.

I was still on the fence about him. I knew I had to make a decision before the night was over because I have my one date rule: He's either a "Go" or a "Stop" after one night. If I go with my gut, which is usually right, I only need about ten minutes. Judge me if you will, but it's worked for me so far. Well, I'm still single so maybe I should retract that last statement.

He insisted on paying the whole check, and we went in search of a place that had German wine because he really wanted me to try some. He was very "classy, classy" and I was fine with it, but I could tell I was not as impressed as some of his previous dates had been. We strolled along the pier looking for the perfect place. We finally settled on an upscale bar near my home. The crowd was "chi-chi" and older, and he seemed right at home. I kept thinking I might need a guy who likes a good cheeseburger and fries. Unlike his previous girlfriends, I eat carbohydrates and I don't throw them up afterward either. After more talk about all of his finer qualities, it was killing me and I had to ask him, "Dave, do people ever ask you if you're ... um ... well ... ah ... gay?"

With a big proud smile he says, "Of course, every day ... but really I'm just a metrosexual." "A what?" I asked. "A metrosexual," he said matter-of-factly, "is a guy who has gay tendencies but likes women. I mean, so what if I like fine dining and have over a hundred pairs of shoes and a personal shopper at Macy's? So what if I'm a good dancer?" Wow! You learn something new every day!

We then got into this conversation about dos and don'ts of dating. He told me his biggest turn off was when a girl shows up wearing a brown belt and black shoes. All I could think about was the brown belt lying on my bed that I almost wore. He told me his mother was a fashion model and she taught him all about the importance of clothes. He also said he had fourteen pairs of jeans. I was dying inside. This was just comical and my mind drifted to thoughts about what the dating world had to offer. Amazing, non-Christian guys who fit all my criteria and Christian guys with personal shoppers? Lord, help me please!

I wanted to actually set Dave up with my friend Trista because she'd be all for this guy. This girl basically owns half of Pottery Barn. She had a tree-trimming party for Christmas but wouldn't let anyone touch the tree. When I go to her apartment I have to pray first that I don't spill on her white couches or white carpet. She and I are like the Odd Couple. If we ever lived together, it could be a reality show to see who would be the first to kill the other with our decorating. So I thought about trying to set them up, but I knew this night was not the time to bring it up.

I did my time, smiled a lot, and we called it a night around eleven thirty. He drove me home and I was hoping to avoid some awkward moment. I mumbled, "You don't have to walk me to my door, I'm fine right here … this was fun … blah, blah …" He smiled, and before I knew it he had planted a kiss on my cheek. A little chill ran up my spine; it had been so long since anyone had kissed me. I kinda liked it, but I think we both realized we weren't a match. I got out of the car and came home to my apartment realizing I had nicely survived another night in the LA dating jungle. I would live to see another day.

63

settling ... a little

So we left off with our heroine having a milestone birthday and an early mid-life crisis, which resulted in her signing back on the Christian dating sites and "waiting on God proactively"—*again*. Okay, so the heroine is me—let's talk.

I was sick of it. I had preached and preached about waiting on God, but I was *so over* the waiting part. I kept hearing all these success stories and even well-known pastors endorsing these Christian dating sites. So I gave in; I put my pics up there and everything. Glamour head shots, of course. One guy wrote me, "What's with the head shots? Are you missing an arm?" You know you can't mess around when it comes to making a first impression. I did my funny profile revealing just enough about me, but not enough to make it seem like I really cared. I then proceeded to peruse the profiles of all the eligible bachelors in my state. I wasn't going out of a twenty-mile radius after my last Canadian online affair. I was older and more serious. I wanted to find my husband and thought technology might help me. I prayed much more diligently this time. I told God I felt at peace about this because I was in a much different place. The minute I didn't feel peace about it, I would stop. Ha! Famous last words!

So it started again. I won't bore you with all the stories and the emails I received. I got everything from overt marriage proposals to dumb opening lines more suitable for bars on the Hermosa Pier. This wasn't as appealing as it was the last time, but don't think I was giving up. Not wanting to be alone in this, I had talked four of my closest friends into this venture with me. We laughed because we'd all get emails from the same guys. One guy wrote my friend Trista and then me. I'm not one to miss an opportunity, so I called him on it and told him she was a nice girl if she would just give up her job at Hooters. She got me back by writing some other guy and saying I was a nice girl as long as I took my medication. As you can see, I wasn't taking this too seriously. I had many email conversations but nothing to write home about.

One guy and I emailed back and forth for almost a month. I liked his picture and vice versa, so finally we agreed to meet. On paper this really worked; he had a really good job and liked the arts and Southern California. He talked about dining at places I had only dreamed of. This seemed very attractive to me. He was Christian as well.

We spoke on the phone and I invited him to a comedy show. He showed up, and when I saw him after the show he looked exactly like his pictures—handsome and sweet. In that instant I could have told you the chemistry was not there, but I was trying to grow and be more mature, so I decided to give him a chance. My friends met him and said he was sweet. We'll call him Bob.

We went out to dinner a couple of times, and for whatever reason I always seemed to be tired when I was around him. I didn't chalk it up to boredom, but I'd find myself checking my watch a lot. Bob was traditional and reliable: called when he said he would, did some nice things for me, and was always polite and respectful of me.

He did have strong faith, but he wasn't really passionate about living it out in his everyday life. He also was really into animals and for that reason alone I should have cut it off. But I was so needy I was even open to meeting his two—count 'em, two—dogs! I started quizzing my friends to ask if chemistry could actually develop. They all overwhelmingly said yes. So I tried ... I really did. He had all the qualities I said I wanted ... except he didn't make me laugh. I wasn't even cracking jokes when we were together; I seemed to be some stiff version of myself. I knew he was attracted to me, and he told me physical appearance was important to him. He was handsome but there was no part of me that even wanted him to hold my hand. On our fourth date I knew it wasn't ever going to happen. I barely got through dinner, I was so bored! I made it to a respectable eleven o'clock, gave him a quick hug goodbye, and got the heck out of there.

I called the girls on the way home ... bummed out! "I tried," I told them, "I really did." From that point forward I would never again *not* trust my gut. God made me this way for a reason. I take it as a time-saver.

64

planes, trains, and chocolate chip cookies

The night after I ended it with Bob I had to pack for my gig in Ohio with three male comics. I knew them—one was my mentor and the other two were acquaintances in the business. I arrived at the airport bright and early, looking haggard to say the least. No makeup!

In fact my skin was all broken out because I had a facial that weekend, and we know how that goes, right? But I wasn't there to impress anyone until I got on stage, so I threw on a hat and pink sweats and went to the airport. These sweats are my fav pink velour ones and my friends think they are an eyesore, but they're comfortable for flying.

My mentor, Terrance, was the headliner, so he was in first class. He told me to go sit in the back with the other comedian whom we'll call Ron because that is his real name. Now I had met Ron about eight months before at a comedy show and had even gone on a date with his best friend some time before that. We'll call his friend Jesse (not his real name). He's really a great guy, but we didn't have any chemistry.

So it's eight o'clock Sunday morning and Ron had just quit his day job the night before to do comedy full-time, and he arrived on the plane with an entire box of Krispy Kreme doughnuts! Not one or two but a whole box! Well, at least sitting next to him would have its advantages!

Before the plane even took off, the antics began. He's telling stories and I'm laughing ... crying actually. We were so loud, I thought we'd get kicked off the plane. We were being like two little kids making jokes at the expense of practically everyone on the plane —including ourselves, of course. It was fun. More than fun, it was relaxing and simply great.

We shared doughnuts and even though he bought me headphones for the movie, I never put them on because I was more than entertained by his quick wit. Can you believe I passed on George Clooney for a Korean/Irish comedian? Well, I did. I don't recall exactly what we talked about, but he told a lot of stories about his dating experiences. Seems he was always "the nice guy," and that didn't work out so well. I asked him what he was looking for in a woman. He said, "Someone who has caller ID and still takes my calls!" He said he didn't have time for a girlfriend because he was really trying to focus on his career right then.

Ron's humor reminded me of Woody Allen, except that he was a Christian. Not only was he Christian, but he was actually living it out in his life. No way! Funny and Christian? I didn't think those guys existed, but then again ... he was a comic! Ron was a perfect gentleman and insisted on carrying my luggage. It wasn't that he was into impressing me; I could just tell he was the kind of thoughtful guy who did those types of things for everyone.

I didn't think much of it until after we all were settled in at the hotel. I went to my room and I was shaking and said to God, "I don't know what's going on here, Lord, but the possibility exists that I may be getting a crush on this comedian guy, and I need you to take care of it because this is not on my agenda! I prayed for an accountant or someone with a 401k plan who could support my lifestyle! This guy totally doesn't even want to date right now! Plus we're in the same circles. This would get really messy! I'm done with drama!" That night it was hard to go to sleep. I kept replaying my conversations with Ron over in my head and giggling to myself.

The next morning we met in the common area to go to breakfast, and it was just the two of us. Somehow we got on some tangent and started up with our antics and campfire stories again, and the morning turned into afternoon. We were still sitting there talking when my mentor came back to get us for lunch. I felt like I was a kid in trouble. Was it written all over my face that after all this time I was becoming smitten with Ron?

I hung on his every word. He made me laugh out loud, but he also had this sweet side to him that I had never seen before. We spent five hours just sitting there talking, and this time we told some more serious stories about our childhoods, our families, and many other topics. This guy was actually funnier and quicker than any guy I had ever met, but unlike my exes in the past, he never resorted to that sarcastic banter that can get mean-spirited. There was an intelligence about him that was becoming more appealing every minute. I was starving, but I didn't want to get up because I was having so much fun just hanging out with Ron.

There I was in another state looking homely with my face all broken out and falling for this guy who had *no idea*. No clue. To him I was this comedy buddy who liked his material ... or was I? I wasn't about to blow my cover with him.

I was starting to become flustered. I was the only girl on this trip, and I had no girlfriend to discuss this with. All these feelings were surfacing, and I really didn't know how to deal with them. Dare I say I was getting goose bumps? All I know is that that afternoon I was following him around the mall like a schoolgirl, tagging along to get pretzels after lunch.

We were laughing and joking and ended up in the bookstore. It was pre-Valentine's Day and all the shelves were filled with love books. We couldn't help but ridicule them. Our running joke was that Kerri didn't have a valentine and we needed to get her one. It was hilarious because we'd take these books, read them aloud, and then act them out, much to the dismay of the people that worked there. Picture me in my winter coat and sweater reading chapter 3 in *How to Strip for Your Husband: A Step-by-Step Guide.* "Step one," I said, swinging my scarf over my head, "Set the mood ... take your right arm and raise it diagonally ..." You get the picture. It was a full show and I was in rare form, but all he seemed to care about was where the new *Green Lantern* comic books were.

We made fun of the horoscope love guides; we cast love spells on each other, and I was truly having the most fun I could imagine having anywhere. Next, I found myself upstairs in the comic book section with him, still just having a grand time. Then it was on to the knitting section and so on. Everything was interesting, whether we were making crazy jokes or discussing the value of knitting. I knew we had a show that night, but I didn't want this time alone with him to end. I knew I had to go do my hair and makeup, but I wanted to hang out with him as long as I could.

Ron knew I liked chocolate so we ended up in the Nestlé's Toll House cookie store. Dude, this guy ate lunch ... then pretzels ... then chocolate chip cookies? He was cool!

It was then that it really hit me ... I liked him. I really liked him. This guy could take me to McDonald's and sit in the sandbox, and not only would I go but we'd have a great time. I'd rather be in a sandbox with him than in some fancy restaurant with any other guy. I knew I was in trouble and my mind just started racing about how much fun it would be to actually go on a date with him back in LA. I couldn't stop myself and it was obvious he had no idea how I felt.

Although we were totally connecting, I assumed he thought I was just another great comedy buddy. I was doing all the flirting I could and was hitting a brick wall. I found myself doing things I would never do. I would reach for his arm when we joked. I would find reasons to be next to him whenever possible. I had not tried this hard in a very long time to get a guy's attention, and it still wasn't working. I must be getting old, I thought.

I couldn't let Ron go. I mean he appreciated the finer things in life like Nestlé's Toll House cookies and the value of a fine bookstore striptease performance. But none of the love spells I cast seemed to be working. I'm glad I didn't pay for that book!

Jesse did a very funny set that night. I thought maybe I could set him up with one of my girlfriends because he was Christian. Then Ron went up and did a set. I remember thinking not only that he was hysterically funny, but that something about him was really attractive to me even though he wasn't what I considered my type (being a non-investment banker comic).

I knew it was bad when after the show about ten of us went out to dinner and I was literally sad that I didn't get to sit next to him. I kept praying about this to God, and he was the only one in the world who knew what was going on with me. I'm sure he was having a ball watching me throw myself at this guy to no avail.

After dinner the comedians were all sitting around talking about the show. I had not had one of my finer performances. I was flustered in so many ways, and I had no one but God to discuss this with. But then I turned to my trusty friend, the computer. As I sat there listening to shop talk, at least I could email my girlfriends back in California and tell them I was losing my mind in frustration. My emails were incoherent ramblings, which mostly started with the word, "Help!" I knew we were leaving tomorrow and reality would set in.

I stayed up till four in the morning with those guys as I sat at my computer trying to make conversation or get some clue from Ron that any of my flirting had registered in his male brain. All that kept coming out of my mouth at that point were ramblings. "Stupid, stupid, stupid," I'd mutter under my breath. When they asked me what was wrong I'd just mutter more and keep emailing ... "Men! You're all so dumb ... I just can't believe you ..." They thought it was some "girl thing" and basically ignored me.

At one point I was staring right at Ron from across the room, and since he was not responding to my thought waves, I wrote him some funny, ranting email about men and how dumb they were. At the end I told him I thought he was cute and that he owed me dinner. One of my tactics was to tell him I wanted to try Korean food, and being that he was Korean, he should offer to take me sometime.

If that wasn't blatant, then I don't know what was. I might as well have written, "Do you like me? Check *Yes* or *No.*" It was late and I didn't care anymore. He would read it back in California, and that's all I could do at that point.

When the subject of dating was brought up by one of the other guys, they began to grill me as I was the only girl present. Ron chose to just smile and remain completely silent on the matter. I was throwing out innuendos left and right, and he sat there happily watching *The Goonies* on television! *The Goonies* ... one of my favorite movies ... see? We had so much in common! I would have been content just to sit next to him and watch the movie, but of course that didn't happen. I finally gave up and went to my room ... exhausted and flustered.

I had a long talk with God that night and was basically saying things like, "Pllleeease God, let him like me! Would that be so terrible? I mean, you did this in the first place. I didn't like him before this trip, and I didn't manipulate anything. Can he please like me back?" I'd been praying this prayer since third grade when I liked Anthony Policello ... but somehow this seemed different. I kept saying, "I know you're not the God of 'just kidding,' and if you start something there has to be a reason. Couldn't this be because you want Ron and me to date? I'll be good, I promise. He's a real Christian, God, and he has all these great qualities, and he's not even my type, and I'm not his, but for whatever reason I have these strong feelings. I'm assuming they are from you. Couldn't you throw a few his way too?"

I was talking to God more like an earthly father. In some ways I felt really close to him because I felt like he was intimately involved with what I was going through. Of course, he's been there patiently waiting to step in and help me out the whole time, but there have been so many situations when I've basically ignored his presence. This was not one of those times. I'd never felt his involvement more, and I was reaching to him directly for guidance. I told him if these feelings were *my* doing only, then he could take them away immediately. I also could see the possibility of getting hurt badly by Ron, and I was not excited about that happening either. I think not knowing was the worst. If he gave me the "friend speech," I could at least cry and then get over it, but I had no idea what was going through his mind.

I slept for three hours that night and then woke up to catch the early morning plane. Our trip home had a connecting flight, and all I could hope was that I'd get to sit by Ron on one of the two. What was this—a sixth grade field trip and I'm saving seats on the school bus? That's how I felt. We got to sit together on the initial flight and even though we were exhausted, we talked the whole time. He went on to tell me *more* stories of his exes and his adventures in Dating Land. Didn't he know this was killing me? He did all these crazy, wonderful things for these other girls and there I was sitting and listening to it all. He did things for other girls I'd only dreamed guys would have done for me ... flowers ... trips to the theater ... new surprise dresses ... candles ... the whole bit!

I finally said, "Ron, I don't want to hear about your exes anymore. This is not therapy!" You know what this guy says? "Okay, okay ... but there was this one time in kindergarten and I had this crush on one girl and we got to get the milk together ..." He was so charming and funny that I gave in.

His storytelling ability was like mine. He could create the setting and tell it like it just happened yesterday; you couldn't help but be entertained. Once again I found myself laughing out loud and getting stares from other tired passengers. They literally turned around and stared at us as if we were two kids whose volume levels needed to be adjusted to our "inside voices."

I knew I made him laugh too. That gave me great joy. He may have dated all these other girls but how many of them were funny? I mean really funny, not just in that laugh-at-his-jokes funny. I knew I could keep up with his wit and he knew it too. Now the question was whether guys actually find that attractive, or was it mildly threatening? He said he wanted to date a funny girl ... but not one funnier than him. I quipped back, "Well then, it could never work between us!" He smiled and laughed out loud.

As we boarded the second plane, Ron took it upon himself to point out the cute guys I could sit next to. He found one in a white cowboy hat to be particularly interesting for me, and we ended up doing a whole routine on cowboys. If he was going to pick them out for me, I was sure going to play along and seem excited.

Of course, we ended up sitting together and amusing ourselves by telling the stewardess we had just met on the first plane and that he had asked me to continue on to Maui with him to visit his pig farm. This woman totally believed us because we were that good, and it was hilariously fun.

About an hour into the flight I was in the back of the plane and the stewardess, who was the first female I had been in personal contact with in quite some time, was asking me about Ron. I fessed up and kinda spilled my guts in this ten-second rant. I said in that total sixth grade way, "Isn't he the cutest thing ever? I like him and he has no idea. I have to go back up there—I only have three hours and twelve minutes to make this work." I was swooning and she was laughing. I was going on almost no sleep and had used my "A-game" all weekend; I had nothing left. I resigned myself to ramblings about how men don't ever get women's signals and how some women seem to like one type of guy but really like another and blah, blah, blah. Did I have to spell it out for him on the food tray in peanuts? I LIKE YOU, YOU FOOL!

We were sitting so close together and all I wanted was for him to put his arm around me or something. I knew that hell would host the Winter Olympics before that would ever happen, so I gave in. I couldn't stay away anymore. I put my head on his shoulder—whether he liked it or not—and fell asleep. At least I could enjoy a few quiet minutes cuddling up next to him. I just told him to be still and he was. It was great ... nice ... comfortable. I had given up trying to convince him of anything. God would have to do something because I was out of tricks.

Well, it was quiet bliss. I slept for about ten minutes on his shoulder and as I woke up I didn't want to move. There was no joking, no stories of exes—just me cuddled up close to this amazingly funny, sweet, caring guy who had no idea how smitten I was with him. I remember trying to actually listen to hear his heart beat ... was it accelerated? I had no luck. He seemed perfectly calm to me.

He had always had girls in his life that liked him. I knew this because I had the pleasure of hearing all his stories. Little did he know that I had a mind like a steel trap, and all of these little details were stored in my memory. I'm not the jealous type, but I was actually jealous of these girls he dated—the ones he wrote poems for, bought flowers for, took to plays and other events. I wanted to be one of those girls. Okay, I wanted to be "the girl," but it didn't seem to me like that was going to happen, so I enjoyed the time with him while it lasted.

It's funny how unglamorous the whole weekend actually was. We were out in the cold in sweat pants. He actually saw me in the red flannel pajamas with rainbows that my grandma had given me for Christmas. I wasn't enticing in any way the whole weekend. In fact, I wasn't even that funny on stage. All I had going for me was a knockout striptease performance in Barnes & Noble and a lot of determination. I've always done whatever it takes to get what I wanted out of life.

Ron never reached out to hold my hand or gave me any signals. He quietly sat next to me as I slept on his shoulder. That was all. We stayed like that till the plane landed. The cute stewardess looked at me with a knowing smile as we taxied in. We were talking and found ourselves to be almost the last people on the plane. Getting off that walkway was going to be the end of something really special … or was it the beginning? I didn't know.

65

she likes you

The entire weekend I was hanging out with Ron, my mentor-comedian friend, Terrance, kept teasing us, making lovebird jokes because he knew something was up. I wasn't about to admit it and obviously Ron wasn't either. I just denied it. I had this little secret that other people didn't know about, and it was kind of special to me. At least that is how I felt about things. I mean we did have a lot at stake. We were both Christian comedians, running around in the same social and professional circles. The last thing we needed was any gossip about us offstage. My whole onstage persona centers around the fact that I'm single. He talks about dating too. If we ever got together it could ruin both our acts! All these thoughts were running through my head as reasons Ron would not be calling me after this weekend. I was sure he wanted to keep business as business.

When we got our bags after the infamous flight, Ron offered to carry mine. We were about to get in separate cabs. I knew he had an expensive ride ahead of him back to his apartment and my car was just minutes away. I took a risk and offered to drive him home. He said okay, as long as he paid my cab fare to my car. It was a deal. I was beyond tired, but I couldn't bear the thought of saying goodbye to him ... not just yet.

All the way home we joked. Yes, he still talked fondly of one ex or another. It's like I knew these girls by now. I'm surprised I just didn't haul off and sock him one in the face and tell him to shut up because I was in such a tired and emotionally spent state. I resisted. He asked me questions about dating and what I liked to do on dates. We did have a lot of things in common — from interests to belief systems.

He was teasing me about having to go back to my day job selling cell phones, and at one point he offered to help me do some filing if I needed it. I was trying to get him to come help me set up my computer monitor and my new VCR. He said he was good at that stuff. That would at least be an excuse to see him again. I had thrown out as many options as I could, and after a long hug goodbye he said, "If you need help with the filing, I wasn't kidding." I said, "No thanks. But maybe you could help with that cooking we were talking about?" He just smiled and I drove away. Frustrated doesn't even begin to describe what I was feeling. I thought I might spontaneously combust.

It was the middle of the day and I needed backup. I needed to talk to "the girls." Whoever answered first was going to get a mouthful. I can't even remember who it was … Gina Miller, I think. I could barely talk — all I could do was swoon; besides, I was delirious at this point from lack of sleep. I tried to relay the story to her but it was worthless. It was totally my dream weekend and no one could understand what it was like for me because they weren't there. I kept blabbering, "I love him … I love him" in some incoherent voice over the phone, half asleep and trying to drive.

I walked into my apartment feeling like I had just arrived home from summer camp. I was exhausted on all levels. I plopped down on my bed, unable to work or do anything but whimper to myself and to God. I just kept thinking about the past weekend and how much fun it was, and why God would give me all these feelings totally out of the blue for a man who probably didn't feel the same way. I prayed, I swooned, and I called friends to relay all the details with my comedic flair for entertainment value. At the end of each conversation I posed the question, "Do you think he likes me?" I was taking a survey and the polls were in my favor.

Of course, I had to call Doug Kligman, my friend from college who left me in the library cubicle, because no matter what, he would tell me how ravishing I was and how dumb any guy would be not to want to move mountains for me. I was feeling old, like I didn't have "the touch" anymore, so I needed some validation. Right on cue Doug says, "I have a really good feeling about this one, Kerri." "You always say that, Doug …" "Yes, but this time it's different, and what you have to do is sit back and wait for him to make his move. Guys want to be the pursuer; don't take that away from him." I said, "What? No way … he's not going to do anything. He's clueless," I cried. I think there was still a part of me that enjoyed the drama of my previous relationships, for it was definitely not as fun as it used to be. Doug at the current time was dating some lovely girl he was head-over-heels for, so his wish for me was to find the same magical connection. He promised me I'd get a phone call by 4:00 p.m. the next day. "And then what?" I asked. "If I don't, will I spontaneously combust? That's almost twenty-four hours! I could die before then from lack of patience and oxygen to my brain!"

So that night at Bible study I asked my friend Suz to pray for me to get my head back on straight and take me out of junior high. We prayed to God to make this whole thing go away if it wasn't his will and to hurry it up if it was. I told God he was, of course, more important than any crush. I didn't like feeling this way, so I needed his help. Immediately I felt peace.

I drifted off to sleep only to be awakened by my cell phone ringing at 10:00 p.m. It was him! I couldn't believe he was calling me. He must have forgotten something in my car. We started chatting like old friends. He didn't say why he was calling and I didn't ask. He was at a comedy club, hanging out and waiting for his friend who was flirting with some girl, so he and I got to chat for a long while. We joked about his taking the last of the chocolate chip cookies we bought in Ohio. I told him I wanted them delivered back to my doorstep, and while he was there, I had some ironing he could do. He didn't mention getting together; we just said goodnight and hung up as if we had been phone buddies for years.

I went to sleep happy that he called, but still not convinced he was interested in more than a new comedy buddy. I knew I made him laugh and that was probably why he was calling. Now who was being dense? Logically, he had many people he could have called that night, but he called me. So if that wasn't a sign then I don't know what was. But in true female fashion, I wanted more ... like an actual date.

The next day he responded to the email I had sent him while in Ohio. He joked a lot, and at the end wrote a nice paragraph telling me how funny he thought I was and how much he enjoyed working with me. He told me he would take me out for Korean food as I had suggested in my email. He said, "It's not often you get to travel with friends and do shows!" I was flabbergasted! Did he just use the *F* word with me? What? I'm the girl *friend*! I knew it! I knew it! He was putting that in there for a reason — to send me a message that I was on the friend level and that was it. He wanted to go out for Korean food, but as friends! I prayed to God about this and told him to make this stop. I had work to do and didn't have time for this schoolgirl craziness going on in my head. I knew God had a plan for me and if it wasn't Ron then it would be somebody even better. I got on with my day.

That night, Terrance, my comedy mentor, called. He would not stop teasing me about Ron and how we'd make such a great couple. I was not going to budge. I thought the moment I let Terrance know about any of my feelings, the cameras would come out and I'd realize I'd been "punked" like on the reality show with Ashton Kutcher. But after about forty minutes, I finally told Terrance how I felt. He was actually surprised. He didn't think Ron was my type; he was really just having fun and teasing me. I actually had to convince him I was serious. I knew Ron wasn't the usual type of guy I dated, but that didn't matter because I definitely liked him and wanted to get to know him better. So all of a sudden he says, "Hold on. I'm calling you back!" "Why?" I asked. He said, "I'm calling that boy and straightening him out! He has no earthly clue you feel this way; trust me!"

So he calls Ron at midnight and says, "So Dude ... what do you think of Kerri?" His exact response was, "So what are we in — eighth grade? What did she say about me?" and on it went. Finally Terrance says, "Dude, she likes you! I mean she *likes you* likes you!"

Come to find out Terrance was right, and Ron needed to be knocked in the head with a two-by-four. He thought I was only being friendly and he had no concept that any of my flirtations were more than Kerri being funny. Arrrrgh, men! Don't they know? What do we women need to do — wear a sign? Obviously we do! I should sell them; I'd make a million dollars.

So the end result was that he *was* interested, and Terrance gave him his blessing to ask me out. He said, "There is no one that is good enough for Kerri and there is no one good enough for you, so you two should be together. It would be great if that happened."

The next day Ron called and asked me out to a comedy show and to get Korean food. He acknowledged that this was breaking the "day of" rule where you have to give a girl some notice before asking her on a date. I acknowledged that I would make an exception because it was a weekday ... and because I was dying to go out with him. I immediately canceled my plans and then went to get a manicure!

I got dressed for my date and tried on these jeans with a cute sweater. I swear I actually had to put on a different sweater because the first one was a bit sexy and I felt like God was telling me not to wear it. Sometimes I can hear his voice so clearly it's scary, and in those times it's pretty easy to do his will. I opted for a conservative top and off I went.

I offered to pick him up because his car was in the shop. When he got into my car he had a bottle of green tea, some banana chips, and goldfish crackers. I didn't realize until the end of our date that he had brought those for me because earlier I had mentioned that I was hungry. I'm not used to that kind of thoughtfulness, so I didn't even open the bottle of tea the whole time. How sad is that?

We went to Korea Town and I used chopsticks for the first time. We laughed and I was the only blonde in the place. He said he would get accolades for that in his culture, showing up with a "blonde princess," as he called me. We had fun. It was comfortable even though I was a bit nervous and so was he. We hadn't discussed any of our previous antics and that was fine by me. We joked a lot, but not the whole time. Again, I realized how smart he was, how much I enjoyed listening to him and learning from him. I knew nothing about Korean culture so I learned a lot about it that night, which was really interesting. I also realized I didn't hate dating. When you're with the right person, you can have fun and not be so analytical about what's coming next. We went to the comedy show and then I dropped him off at his home. As he was leaving he pulled out a box; inside was a paper scroll with a bow on top. He said, "Read this when you get home," and he hugged me and got out of the car.

When I arrived home I opened the piece of paper with my heart beating madly, to see that he had written me a silly poem called "A Poem for Poms." It was so sweet and kind and funny! I could barely stand it. Not only had he remembered I didn't drink coffee, he had put together a little care package with lots of tea bags, some Starburst candies he knew I liked, and the last two chocolate chip cookies we bought together at Nestlé's. To say that I was overwhelmed with this man's thoughtfulness is an understatement. I floated off to sleep in total giddiness. For the first time in my life, this felt right on every level … really right.

I remember praying to God, "If this is the kind of man you have for me, God, then I'm sure glad I waited."

66

the end?

In all of these adventures I've shared with you, it would seem that I haven't mastered the art of waiting on God, but I think it's a never-ending process. I'll keep trying and I'll keep falling down, but I'll get right back up again. I didn't want this book to be any kind of "how-to" manual. I hope you've learned as much as I have. No guy, no matter what, is going to solve my problems or make me feel complete. I just know that God had a lot of work to do in my life and the way I looked at things, and I know he still does. My pastor said, "Stop looking for the right person and be the right person!" I always hated that saying. I thought it was ridiculous coming from someone happily married with three kids. But what I think God is really saying is I have to get my heart right with him first.

I am learning that this is the way life goes. I'll never be perfect, but God loves me. He has abundant blessings for me. He has plans for my life, and every day is a new chapter, a new adventure. Only he knows the wonder he has for me around the next corner. He promised to give me the desires of my heart ... and I know God never breaks a promise.

He loves you too. No matter where you are, or what has happened in your past, he will always love you. So the next time you find yourself in some ridiculously silly situation—like pretending to like dogs for a guy or eating too much chocolate after a chick flick—laugh, get over it, and picture God up there laughing *with* you. I figure God loves to laugh or he wouldn't have invented dating in the first place!

Kerri Pomarolli is one of today's fastest rising stars in the Christian arena and is being touted as the Christian Bridget Jones. Her lethal wit keeps audiences of all ages laughing, as she tells of her southern belle mother who's obsessed with seeing her only daughter married, and an Italian father who's watched one too many episodes of the *Sopranos* and tells everyone the family is in the witness protection program!

She is touring the country with her hilarious, yet inspirational comedy routine. As a headliner and featured comedian, Kerri's shows are getting national attention with standing room only at comedy clubs, corporate events, girl's nights out, singles and marriage conferences, colleges, and churches.

Kerri is a veteran of television with credits that include Comedy Central, Lifetime network, ABC, Fox, TBN, CBN, the Total Living Network, and twenty-five appearances on the *Tonight Show with Jay Leno*, among many other television appearances.

She is currently a board member of Breaking into Hollywood, head cowriter and founder of Act In Faith Hollywood Theater Ensemble, and a contributing writer for *Christian Comedy* magazine, along with many other magazines and newspapers. Kerri is a new syndicated cartoonist and creator of the comic strip *KERRI* as well as a contributing writer in Anna Jane Grossman and Flint Wainess's new book, *It's Not Me, It's You*, to be published in February 2006.

She enjoys living by the sea in California with her famous hammock and enjoys meeting her many fans at her speaking engagements. Please visit her website and sign the guest book ... her mother would appreciate it!

www.kerripom.com

For booking or speaking engagements, please contact:

Rhonda Boudreaux

(510) 236-2668

Rdboudreaux1@aol.com

Share Your Thoughts

With the Author: Your comments will be forwarded to the author when you send them to *zauthor@zondervan.com*.

With Zondervan: Submit your review of this book by writing to *zreview@zondervan.com*.

Free Online Resources at
www.zondervan.com/hello

 Zondervan AuthorTracker: Be notified whenever your favorite authors publish new books, go on tour, or post an update about what's happening in their lives.

 Daily Bible Verses and Devotions: Enrich your life with daily Bible verses or devotions that help you start every morning focused on God.

 Free Email Publications: Sign up for newsletters on fiction, Christian.living, church ministry, parenting, and more.

 Zondervan Bible Search: Find and compare Bible passages in a variety of translations at www.zondervanbiblesearch.com.

 Other Benefits: Register yourself to receive online benefits like coupons and special offers, or to participate in research.